MOTORING

A PICTURE HISTORY OF

MOTORING

By L. T. C. ROLT

THE MACMILLAN COMPANY
NEW YORK

FIRST PUBLISHED 1956

Printed in Great Britain

Contents

Preface

To an author accustomed to selecting at the most fifty pictures to illustrate a book, an allowance of more than four hundred and fifty in which to tell the story of motoring seemed at first thought unbelievably generous. Yet it soon became apparent that it was niggardly compared with the size of the subject and that the problem would be, not how to fill the following pages, but what to leave out. This printed picture gallery could be filled three times over with portraits of motor cars alone, yet that would be to tell only half the story. For the word 'motoring' embraces not only the car itself but the use which we have made of it for business, for pleasure or for sport and the changes which the car has brought to the roads on which it runs. The road cannot be left out of a history of motoring any more than a history of railways could be produced without reference to the permanent way and signalling.

It was when I came to consider this aspect of the subject that I realized my ignorance, even of the changes which had taken place during my own motoring career. When and where were the first traffic lights installed, the first white line painted, the first one-way traffic system introduced? I have to confess that I did not know the answers until I had burrowed through files of old press photographs.

The pages which follow are divided into three main sections: first, what might be described as the 'primitive' period up to 1900; next, the years 1900 to 1914 when the motor car grew from infancy to manhood; finally, the years between the two great wars which saw such a vast increase in the output of cars. In each of these sections I have tried to show, not only typical cars and significant developments in design, but also what motoring was like in town, in country and in the realm of motoring sport. I make no apology for devoting the most space to the second of these three sections and for treating more briefly the recent past. I felt justified in dealing fully with a period of such immense significance in the history of motoring at the expense of those later years with which most of those now holding a steering wheel are already familiar and which are better left to the assessment of some future historian.

It has not been possible in the space available to cover transatlantic development fully; the emphasis must necessarily lie in Europe and predominantly in Great Britain. Where the portraits of early cars are concerned I have endeavoured so far as possible, to select contemporary pictures. Authenticity and period atmosphere have been the aims here, for there are few survivors of the past that have not been modified in some degree if only by the fitting of number plates or of a more modern type of tyre. Experts may enjoy spotting the few exceptions to this rule.

It is only in recent years that the value of old photographs and other early motoring records has come to be properly appreciated. In searching for material for this book it was heartbreaking to discover how much had been dispersed or destroyed. This makes the surviving material the more precious and prompts the question whether a national collection of motoring records should not be established in this country. At present, aside from the Library of the Veteran Car Club, the *Picture Post* Library, and certain private collections, the student must needs worry the manufacturer or the motoring press, but in America it is otherwise. There, under what is called 'the Farmington Plan', the larger Public Libraries are encouraged to specialize in subjects appropriate to their location, and any relevant material which becomes available is routed to them. So it comes about that the Public Library of Detroit boasts an Automotive History Collection which must be second to none. Should not a similar collection be formed at Coventry, the cradle of our automobile industry?

A list of formal acknowledgments appears at the end of this book but I should like to add a note of personal thanks to all those who assisted me so generously in the collection of this material. First, those who helped me from across the Atlantic: my friend H. Austin Clark, Junior, Mr Peter S. de Beaumont, Mr Walter J. Conaty of the Detroit Public Library, the pioneer automobilist Charles B. King, and Mr Smith Hempstone Oliver of the Transportation Section of the Smithsonian Institution at Washington. Next, my motoring friends in this country and especially the following: Messrs Ronald Barker, Peter Garnier, Anthony Heal, Kent Karslake, John Morley, Laurence Pomeroy and Stanley Sears. Finally, I would pay tribute to those motor manufacturers who supplied pictures and to those members of the staffs of *The Autocar, The Motor* and the *Picture Post* Library without whose willing labours on my behalf the compilation of this book would have been quite impossible.

L.T.C.R.

I

* The Horseless Carriage *

1769-1900

A HORSELESS CARRIAGE! The internal combustion engine is a comparatively recent invention, but the idea of using some form of mechanical power to propel a carriage on the road had haunted the mind of man for centuries before it was successfully realized. It was the application of steam power in the eighteenth century which first provided a practical means of propulsion and Nicholas Joseph Cugnot of France was the first man to harness it successfully in a full-sized vehicle.

In 1803, Richard Trevithick built his London steam carriage and for the next forty years England held the initiative in this branch of engineering. Trevithick was the pioneer of high-pressure steam and, using a small Cornish type boiler working at 60 lb. pressure, his London carriage was the first road vehicle expressly designed to carry passengers to operate successfully. It was followed by many other steam vehicles large and small which ran with varying success and of which only a few examples are illustrated here. Today we should consider them highly unreliable and dangerous, but

9

considering the circumstances it is remarkable that they performed as well as they did. Roads were rutted and rough, suspension and steering systems crude, rubber tyres were unknown and instead of high-tensile steels only cast or wrought iron was available so that breakages were frequent.

Although Rudolph Ackermann in 1818 took out an English Patent for the modern system of steering by pivoting the two front wheels independently, it was not adopted by the carriage builders of the day. Some, to obviate the heavy and dangerous pivoting axle, used a single front wheel, while others turned the pivoting axle by means of a leading pilot wheel. The large Gurney coach illustrated here has two of these leading wheels and is therefore, in effect, an articulated six-wheeler. The connecting rods frequently drove a cranked rear axle or crank pins on the driving wheels which meant that the machinery was partially unsprung, and was therefore subjected to fearful stresses and strains leading to dire disintegrations. Boilers were another source of trouble. Cugnot's carriage could only run for twenty minutes before it must needs stop for an equal length of time to regain steam pressure, and later designers faced the same difficult choice between an inordinately heavy boiler and a lighter unit of limited capacity. The usual compromise was a boiler in which the margin of safety was perilously small owing to the desire to save weight. When such a unit was subjected to the stresses of a road carriage the reason for the explosion of Scott Russell's steam coach and similar disasters can be easily understood.

Another problem which confronted these early builders was the strain set up in the driving axle when turning corners. Some drove on one wheel only, some on both wheels independently, and some used systems of clutches or ratchets and pawls, while others (such as the Yarrow & Hilditch illustrated here) used an extremely narrow or 'crabbed' rear track and hoped for the best. Of English builders only Roberts, in 1833, built a carriage incorporating the differential gear which solved this problem and is now a commonplace of automobile design. But, like Trevithick before him, Roberts died in poverty.

Despite their crudity these early vehicles achieved some remarkable performances. The Summers & Ogle coach, working at 250 lb. pressure, touched 32 m.p.h. with a full load, while that built by Hill of Dartford ran from London to Hastings and back, 128 miles in the day, in 1841. In 1861, The Earl of Caithness drove his Rickett light steamer over the Ord of Caithness. 'We rose a thousand feet in about five miles', said the Earl afterwards, 'but I got over without trouble. There is no difficulty in driving a steam carriage on the common roads'.

But such feats would remain unsurpassed until the end of the century, for a preoccupation with railways, punitive tolls on the turnpikes and finally legislation which banished from the road all but heavy agricultural engines, killed initiative in England. The feats of these first pioneers were forgotten so completely that many of their inventions had to be 're-invented' when interest in road vehicles revived.

It was in France that that revival took place, its leading exponents being Amédée Bollee, Count de Dion and M. Bouton, and Leon Serpollet, the great exponent of the 'flash' steam generator and, later, of the use of liquid fuel. Between them an altogether lighter type of steam vehicle was evolved. But in Lenoir's and Otto's 'gas' engines a

10

new source of motive power had already appeared and had been successfully embodied in road vehicles in Germany by Carl Benz and Gottlieb Daimler. French engineers soon recognized the advantages of an engine that required no boiler or water tanks, and with the exception of Serpollet, they turned their attention to the new power.

In the series of competitions and races held on the roads of France between 1894 and 1900 the motor car was born and on those same roads it was brought to perfection in the next decade. It was largely due to the stresses of competition so fierce that only the fittest machine could survive that, once launched upon the world, the motor car developed with such astonishing rapidity, a mechanical monstrosity becoming a reliable and widely accepted form of transport in a few years.

The first motor competition ever organized, the Paris-Rouen Trial of 1894, produced an extraordinary variety of entries. Not only vehicles propelled by petrol, steam and electricity but by 'hydraulics', 'compressed air', 'system of levers', 'system of pendulums' and, strangest of all, 'Combination of animate and mechanical motor'. But these freaks were never in the picture, while electricity was soon eliminated because of its limited range. The issue became a straight fight between petrol and steam with the latter heavily outnumbered.

The first Benz and Daimler cars mounted their engines horizontally in the rear and vertically amidships. Carl Benz clung obstinately to his arrangement with drive by belts and chains, but the system which proved itself the best in the French road races of the nineties was that of the Panhard et Levassor. This consisted of a vertical two, or later four, cylinder engine mounted at the front and driving the rear wheels via a clutch and sliding change speed gears. The differential of the Panhard was mounted on a counter-shaft which drove the rear axle through chains and sprockets. But in 1894 the brothers Renault built their first car with a 'live' rear axle, while in the following year the brothers Michelin ran the first car to be fitted with pneumatic tyres. Thus, albeit crudely, nearly all the basic principles of what would eventually become the orthodox design of the motor car had been evolved in France before the turn of the century.

Meanwhile in America, far removed from the Continent, engineers were pursuing independent lines of research and experiment which were to produce some strange results before the orthodox layout was finally adopted. In England, as the following pictures show, there was no lack of enthusiastic pioneers though their efforts were ham-strung by repressive legislation. Although the so-called 'Red Flag Act' was repealed in November 1896, the motorist was still subject to a severe speed limit while races on public roads were, of course, forbidden. The pioneers celebrated the repeal by the famous run to Brighton, but it is safe to say that until the end of the century the average man in the street was unaware of the revolution that was taking place on the roads of Europe and looked upon the 'horseless carriage' as a rich man's toy. It was not the Brighton Run but the great 1,000 miles trial organized by the Automobile Club (soon to become the *Royal* Automobile Club) in 1900 which first made the people of Britain realize that a new form of transport had definitely arrived. So far as this country was concerned it marked a turning point. Overcoming the initial handicap, the British Motor Industry would surpass the finest products of Europe within the next decade.

11

2. Joseph Cugnot was the first man in the world to run a full sized horseless carriage on the road (1769). When this, his second carriage, overturned at a street corner in Paris, both the luckless inventor and his machine were imprisoned.

3. (*Right*) Trevithick's London Road Carriage, 1803.

4 & 5. Sir Goldsworthy Gurney's steam coach of 1830, seen here at Hyde Park Corner, operated a regular service between Gloucester and Cheltham for four months carrying a total of 3,000 passengers. Its weight was $1\frac{1}{2}$ tons, speed 8/10 m.p.h. Gurney later made a light steam drag to take place of carriage horses. In the above engraving (which does not show mechanical details) Gurney is driving with Robert Stephenson beside him. the carriage are the Hon. Mrs Arbuthnot, Mrs Maberley, Lord Fitzroy Somerset and (standing) the Duke of Wellington.

6. Colonel Maceroni's steam carriage, 1833. A remarkable performer among early carriages which covered a considerable mileage in the London area and later in Paris. Two-cylinder engine, vertical multi-tubular boiler with forced draft by fan, 150 lb. pressure. Speed 20 m.p.h.

7. Disaster: The weakness of all the early steam carriages was the boiler. This purports to be an eye-witness' impression of the explosion of John Scott Russell's coach following the breakage of a wheel near Paisley, July 29th 1834. Five passengers died in this, the first fatal accident to a mechanically-propelled road vehicle in Britain.

8. Walter Hancock's steam coaches, 1826-36. Hancock was the most successful builder and operator of steam carriages of the period. His fleet worked a regular service between the City and Paddington. *Automaton*, the last and most successful of his ten vehicles, achieved 21 m.p.h.

9. Few steam vehicles were built in England after 1840 owing to pre-occupation with railways and opposition from Turnpike Trusts. This light steam carriage of 1859 by Thomas Rickett of Buckingham was a successful exception. The carriage shown is of his later gear-driven type as supplied to the Earl of Caithness who drove it from Inverness to Borrogill Castle over the Ord of Caithness.

10. The Yarrow & Hilditch carriage was another exception. Built by Cowan of Greenwich, it was shown at the London Exhibition of 1862.

11 & 12. This light road steamer, built by Tennants of Leith to the design of R. W. Thompson in 1867, was the first mechanically-propelled vehicle in the world to run on rubber tyres. These, of course, were solid tyres, but as early as 1846 Thompson patented a pneumatic tyre which consisted of a rubberised inner tube and an outer cover of riveted leather segments. One of these tyres, as fitted to a horse brougham, is shown on right. Dunlop was ignorant of Thompson's work when he re-invented the pneumatic tyre for bicycles in 1888.

–16. While development of the steam vehicle in England was crippled by legislation, progress on the Continent continued and produced an together lighter type of vehicle after the introduction of liquid fuel by Leon Serpollet. Top left is 'L'Obéissante', the first steam vehicle built by médée Bollée senior. Coal fired and seating twelve, the front wheels are independently sprung and pivoted. Top right, the Count de Dion is seen on e of his first steam tricycles in 1887. Below, left, Serpollet and Archdeacon are setting out on a run from Paris to Lyons in January 1890. By contrast e English steam vehicle remained heavy and cumbersome as shown (bottom right) by the Clarkson steam barouche of 1898.

17 & 18. The first challenge to steam came in January 1860 when Ettienne Lenoir patented 'an engine dilated by the combustion of gas'. (left). Two years later, Beau de Rochas evolved the four-stroke cycle and Doctor N. A. Otto's famous 'Silent Gas Engine' of 1876 (right) worked on this principle.

19 & 20. To apply the new power to a road vehicle was an obvious step and Lenoir himself is said to have made a horseless carriage of 1½ h.p. i 1862. Siegfried Markus of Mecklenburg built his first car in 1868 and here, beside his portrait, is the car which he exhibited at the Vienna Exhibitio of 1873.

1/24. Carl Benz (left) and Gottlieb Daimler were the first to build the new motor carriages on a commercial scale. Below are the Benz motor tricycle of 1885 with vertical crankshaft and the first four-wheeled Daimler car of 1886. Daimler's partner, Maybach, is seen at the controls with young Paul Daimler beside him.

26. Fernand Forest of Clermont Ferrand built this, the first four cylinder petrol engine, in 1891. With electric ignition and all valves mechanically operated from one camshaft it was far ahead of contemporary engine design.

25. A Daimler light quadricycle of 1889. Once again Wilhelm Maybach is in charge.

27. An historic family outing. The first Panhard et Levassor car of 189 built on Benz lines. M. Levassor drives; behind (prudently armed with a umbrella) M. Panhard endeavours to soothe Madame Levassor's apprehensions.

28. An early Daimler with forward-mounted engine.

PARIS
TO
ROUEN
RACE
1894

29-36. The first motor competition ever held consisted of a run from Paris to Rouen in 1894 organised by *Le Petit Journal*. The event, open to 'propellers of all kinds and carriages of all shapes', attracted a weird and wonderful collection of vehicles, many of which never reached the starting line. Here are some of the more successful competitors. The De Dion steam drag (No. 4) was the first to reach Rouen. M. Vacheron's carriage (No. 24) is noteworthy for its wheel steering, the only example in the event.

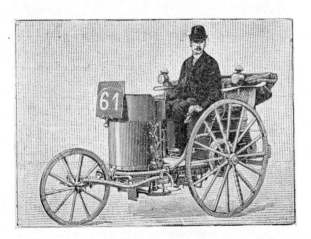

37-40. More competitors in the Paris-Rouen Run of 1894.

41. Unprotected by hood or windscreen, the pioneer auto-mobilist dressed like an Arctic explorer and frequently presented a terrifying appearance when, in addition, he was be-goggled or masked. Here is the celebrated *peau de bique* or goatskin coat made fashionable by the Chevalier Renee de Knyff.

42. Frank Hedges Butler in a Benz of 1898.

43. The famous No. 5 Panhard which won the Paris-Bordeaux-Paris Race of 1895. M. Levassor drove the whole distance of 732 miles in 48 hrs. 48 mins., an average of 14.91 m.p.h. It was an epic of endurance. These two cars make an interesting contrast. While Benz clung obstinately to the horizontal engine at the rear, Panhard had adopted a forward mounted Phènix two-cylinder vertical engine driving through clutch and gearbox. The success of the Panhard design determined the lines on which the automobile would develop.

& 45. Not Charlie Chaplin but Louis Renault in his first car. On right is another Renault which claims to be the first car with enclosed drive. The Renault brothers were the first to employ a 'live' rear axle with shaft drive instead of belts or chains.

46. The first car to be fitted with pneumatic tyres. Dunlop held that pneumatics would not stand the weight of the new vehicles but Michelin thought otherwise and entered his Peugeot 'L'Eclair' in the Paris-Bordeaux-Paris race of 1895. The large box at the back carried tools and spares. After persistent tyre troubles Michelin gave up the struggle at Rouen on the return journey but the superiority of the car when running had proved his point.

47-49. Left: The long and the short of it: The Count de Dion and Monsieur Bouton in consultation in their laboratory at Puteaux. Turning from steam to petrol the two pioneers built cars and the successful motor tricycle shown here. But their most notable contribution was the single cylinder, 'high-speed' engine (top). In air or water-cooled form this engine powered many of the early light cars built in France, England and America.

52. In these early days electricity as well as steam challenged the petrol car. At the top, Camille Jenatzy is seen at the tiller of his famous electric racer 'La Jamais Contente' after raising the World's Flying Kilometre record to 65.79 m.p.h. at Achères on April 29th 1899. Jenatzy thus became the first man to exceed a mile a minute and 100 k.p.h. on the road. Below left, Thomas A. Edison, the famous inventor, stands beside his first American Baker electric car, while on the right, Walter H. Bersey is seen at the controls of his electric landau which he drove on the Brighton Run of 1896. Bersey was a pioneer builder of electric vehicles in England using motors made by Messrs Elwell Parker of Wolverhampton.

53 & 54. Despite the crippling effect of 'The Red Flag Act' in England, English inventors were not idle. As early as 1887 Edward Butler built a motor tricycle with such advanced features as electric ignition, radiator cooling and Ackermann steering.

55 & 56. The Rootes & Venables car and the car built by J. H. Knight of Farnham (right). Both appeared in 1895.

PROGRAMME

HORSELESS CARRIAGE EXHIBITION,

ORGANISED BY

SIR DAVID SALOMONS.

Tunbridge Wells Agricultural Show Ground,

(KINDLY LENT FOR THE OCCASION),

TUESDAY, OCTOBER THE 15TH, 1895,

FROM 3.0 TO 5.0 P.M.

LIST OF EXHIBITS:

1. CARRIAGE by Messrs. PANHARD and LEVASSOR of Paris, with Daimler Petroleum Engine, shown by kind permission of the Hon. EVELYN ELLIS. This carriage is one of the type of the prize winners in the Paris-Bordeaux race last year.

2. FIRE ENGINE, for a country house, kindly lent by the Hon. EVELYN ELLIS, worked by a Daimler Petroleum Engine, and built by the same makers as the preceding exhibit.

The local Volunteer Fire Brigade, under Capt. Tinne, will give a Demonstration with this Engine, in which Mr. Evelyn Ellis will probably take part.

3. TRICYCLE, worked by Petroleum Motor, with electric spark ignition, shown by Messrs. DE DION & BOUTON of Paris, after the design of Count de Dion and M. Bouton. The weight is about 90 lbs.

4. STEAM HORSE, attached to a carriage, shown by Messrs. DE DION & BOUTON of Paris.

5. TRICYCLE, exhibited by M. GUÉDON, for the Gladiator Cycle Company of France. The horse-power is about two-thirds, the fuel is mineral naptha, and the ignition is by the electric spark. The carboniser, in this motor, is dispensed with. The weight is approximately 112 lbs. The pedals are used to start, but, when the motor runs, the pedals are automatically disconnected.

6. VIS-A-VIS, built by Messrs. PEUGEOT of Paris, fitted with a Daimler Engine, supplied by Messrs. PANHARD and LEVASSOR, and shown by Sir DAVID SALOMONS. The weight of this carriage is 13 cwt., and is intended to run 180 to 200 miles without recharging. The horse-power is 3¾; the speed on a hill of 10 per cent. inclination is about four miles per hour, and on the level fifteen miles per hour, maximum.

(The Hon. Evelyn Ellis, Count de Dion, Baron de Zuylen de Nyevelt de Haar, M. Bouton, Mr. Frederick Simms, M. Guédon, and others who have kindly assisted in this Exhibition are present.)

N.B.—A few other carriages have been promised, but the shortness of the notice renders it doubtful whether they will arrive in time. It was hoped that one or two carriages propelled by electricity would also be on exhibition, but these could not be prepared by the date fixed. The carriages shewn illustrate, however, the chief types in vogue, and are similar to those which won the Paris-Bordeaux Race last year, a distance of between 700 and 800 miles.

Every effort has been made to collect as many carriages as possible, but as the few which are in use are widely scattered, it is difficult to obtain the loan of them, but the carriages exhibited fairly illustrate the development of this means of locomotion to the present date.

7 & 58. Prominent among the English pioneers was Sir David Salomons, first President of the Self-Propelled Traffic Association formed in 1895 to press for the repeal of the 'Red Flag Act'. He organised the first exhibition of cars ever to be held in this country. He is seen (right) at the tiller of his Peugeot 'Vis-à-vis' on the Tunbridge Wells Show Ground.

THE DAIMLER OIL MOTOR

Horseless Carriages

UNDER the direction of the Motor Car Club a practical display of horseless road vehicles was given on Saturday afternoon at the Imperial Institute, in the northern gallery and the adjoining garden. The Motor Car Club is a society for the protection, encouragement, and development of the motor car or horseless carriage industry. It proposes to hold and arrange exhibitions and competitions, and to give premiums and prizes. It takes an active interest in the Bill to be presented in Parliament this Session for the purpose of gaining freedom for the autocar. When that is attained, and autocars are free to circulate without being preceded by danger signals, the club proposes to "develop its social side upon the lines of the Automobile Club of Paris." Four different machines were exhibited. The first, which has been in existence five years, was driven by a Daimler oil motor; the second was made by the Acme Motor Carriage Company, and was also driven by an oil motor; the third was worked by the Kane-Pennington oil engine; and in the fourth electricity was the motive power. All of these were shown in operation, and various tests as to speed, starting, and steering were carried out. The first two machines were also subjected to grade tests in the west garden, where they surmounted easily enough a short slope with a gradient of 1 in 10.

59 & 60. Poster and contemporary account of the first motor exhibition to be held in London, May 1896.

61. Vehicles taking part in a later show at the Agricultural Hall, Islington, July 1899.

62/64. Three more British pioneers. Top: F. R. Simms, pioneer of high-tension ignition and founder member of the R.A.C. and S.M.M.T., seen at the Crystal Palace at the tiller of the first Canstatt Daimler to arrive in this country, 1895. Left: the Hon. C. S. Rolls in the 8 h.p. four-cylinder Panhard et Levassor built to his order in 1898. The car is fitted with pneumatics, and from the look of things Rolls has been experiencing the usual tyre trouble. Above: The Hon. Evelyn Ellis imported his first car before the repeal of the 'Red Flag Act'. Here he is seen at the controls of J. S. Critchley's Daimler on the Malvern Hills.

65–67. On November 14th 1896 the famous London to Brighton Run celebrated the 'emancipation' of the British motorist by the repeal of the 'Red Flag Act'. In the top left picture the cars are proceeding from the Central Hall to the start headed by a Panhard driven by McRobie Turrell, Secretary of the Motor Car Club. The Club President, H. J. Lawson, sits beside him carrying a flag. The top right picture shows the cars passing through Reigate. Below, the Arnold Benz and a Panhard are seen outside the Hotel Metropole, Brighton the following day.

68 & 69. Easily the fastest vehicles on the Brighton Run were the Leon Bollee tricars driven by Amédée Bollee Jun. and his brother Leon. The driver of the example shown here is Charles Jarrott. The intrepid passenger was much nearer the accident than the driver and the cartoon on the right shows what happened to H. O. Duncan's unfortunate companion on the run to Brighton.

70. Among those who took part in the Brighton Run was the American E. J. Pennington on a tricycle of his manufacture. Pennington made mysterious and extravagant claims for his machines and indulged in highly fanciful advertisements such as the above.

71. In advertising his British Motor Company, H. J. Lawson also let his imagination run riot.

72-74. The first practical results of Lawson's activities scarcely lived up to the grandiose prospectus and publicity. The first English-built Daimler (top) was a crude affair, while the Coventry Motette, a direct but inferior copy of the Leon Bollee, was built on premises which were not impressive (centre). As for Lawson's 'Gyroscopic Car' (bottom) it was an aberration with terrifying possibilities of disaster of which nothing more was heard. Lawson's two daughters are seen bravely trying out the mechanical pony.

75-77. Top left: Henry Ford looks at his first car which he built in 1896. Right: First to build cars commercially in America were the brothers Charles and Frank Duryea. This is their first car, now preserved in the National Museum at Washington. It first ran through the streets of Springfield, Mass., in 1893. In 1894 it was fitted with two speed and reverse transmission, the gears being changed by moving the steering tiller vertically. Below: Winner of America's first motor competition. J. Frank Duryea at the tiller of the car which he designed, built and drove in the Chicago *Times Herald* contest on October 31st 1895. Snow and bitter cold made driving conditions appalling and only one other car, the Mueller-Benz, finished the fifty-four miles course.

78. Cars at the Stonebridge Hotel, Motor Car Club's Coventry-Birmingham Run, May 1897. The Conductor of the De Dion steamer seems to be in trouble and the following tricar is enveloped in steam.

79. Frank Butler, Benz, takes a corner on the Hog's Back, Automobile Club's Easter Tour, 1898.

80. The new power brought new dangers. The first fatal accident to a petrol car in England occurred in February 1899 when the rear wheel of this Daimler collapsed while the car was descending Grove Hill, Harrow. Driver and passenger were flung out and killed.

81. Artist H. M. Paget's impression of the Exhibition organised by the Automobile Club in the Old Deer Park, Richmond, June 1899.

82, 83. Not all artists were as kind as Paget, for the struggles and misfortunes of the early autocarists were easy game for the cartoonist. These two drawings form part of a contemporary strip cartoon.

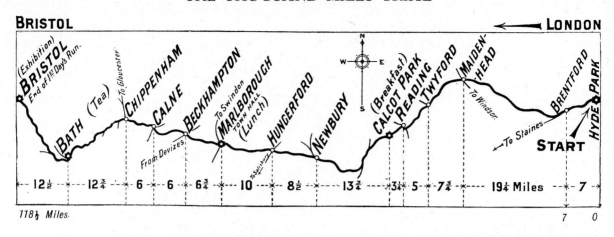

BRISTOL — LONDON →

(Exhibition)
BRISTOL
End of 1st Day's Run.

BATH (Tea)   To Gloucester.   CHIPPENHAM   CALNE   BECKHAMPTON   To Swindon   MARLBOROUGH TOWN HALL (Lunch)   HUNGERFORD   NEWBURY   (Breakfast) CALCOT PARK   READING   TWYFORD   MAIDEN-HEAD   To Windsor.   BRENTFORD   HYDE PARK

From Devizes.   To Salisbury.   To Staines.   START

12½   12¾   6   6   6¾   10   8½   13¾   3¼   5   7¾   19¼ Miles   7

118½ Miles.   7   0

84/86. It was the great 1,000 miles trial of the Automobile Club held in April/May 1900 which first convinced the people of Britain that the new vehicles were practical means of long distance transport and not toys. It was a great milestone in the history of motoring in this country. Above is the first of the route maps issued by *The Autocar* to competitors in the event.

(continued below, right)

In the middle picture the cars are seen leaving Lincoln on their southward journey while below the competitors are lined up in Whitehall after finishing. The leading car, No. A17, is the Panhard driven by the Hon. C. S. Rolls which put up an outstanding performance. Making only one involuntary stop, Rolls won the only gold medal awarded in the event.

87 & 88. Just as sceptics and critics of railways were confounded when Queen Victoria made her first journey from Slough to Paddington in 1842, so, at the end of the century, royal patronage signified that the motor car had now definitely arrived. Above: Edward, Prince of Wales, in Mr Montagu's 12 h.p. Daimler at Highcliffe Castle, 1899. Below: The Duke of York, later King George V, about to leave the Hendre, Monmouth in a Panhard driven by the Hon. C. S. Rolls in 1900. In the back seat, in light bowler, is Rolls' father, Lord Llangattock.

89-93. Advertisements
of 1900.

94/97. Further advertisements of the period.

Cars, etc., For Sale & Wanted.

THE property of a Nobleman. An 8 h.p. Panhard car, with two interchangeable bodies—Mail Phaeton or Siamese, with hood fitting either seat, for sale, a bargain at £650.—The car is in thorough running condition, and is on view at Mulliner's, 28, Brook Street, Bond Street, W.

DE DION 2¼ h.p. Racing Tricycle with special finish, made to the order of Mr. S. F. Edge, brand new English Dunlop tyres, all accessories, in perfect running order; will run 130 miles without recharging ; lubrication from seat while running; price £60.—Can be seen at 14, Regent Street, London.

FOR Sale, 5 h.p. Benz Victoria, with hood and side doors, newly painted, too large for owner; price £155, buying smaller car.—Hargreaves, 26 Padiham Road, Burnley.

INTERNATIONAL Benz, with hood, in good condition, upholstered in leather, starts from seat, fitted with ignition control lever, Brampton chains, and many other improvements, can be seen and tried by appointment; price 95 guineas, a bargain, owner going in for larger car.—Dr. Whitehall-Cooke, 129, Water Lane, Cricklewood.

SEVEN horse-power Phebus-Aster Racing Tricycle, two motors, Longeemare carburettor, guaranteed forty-two miles an hour, very silent, fastest machine in England, holder of English record.—Frank F. Wellington, 36, St. George's Square, Regent's Park, N.W.

BARGAIN.—For sale, small steam motor, waggonette pattern, well seasoned body, fitted with Brampton chains and chain wheels; price £25.—Apply G., 51, Tennyson Road, Penge, S.E.

TWO-SPEED 3 h.p. Benz, in perfect condition, very fast, and excellent hill-climber; price £110, fifty miles trial trip for a *bona fide* purchaser.—Organist, Bexleyheath, Kent.

LIFU Waggonette, perfect order; having improved form of boiler, is well suited for experimental work; any reasonable offer accepted.—H. Graves, Brandon, Suffolk.

FOR Sale, motor car, using heavy oil, patented balance, reversing and speed gear fitted, would sell car and patents, or either separately; engine 3 h.p.—Geering, Rolvenden, Kent.

FOR Sale, Lifu waggonette of great power, splendid order but no boiler, same being used for another purpose; a new boiler could easily be fitted. Price £450.—Apply Z, care of Mr. Green, Stationer, Thetford.

THREE splendid new Panhard-Levassor motor cars for sale. 8 h.p. aluminium racer, very latest model, beautifully upholstered, large Michelin tyres, unpuncturable protectors, £600; 5 h.p. lovely carrosserie, Michelin tyres, £280; also 16 h.p. racer, ready January.—Hon. L. Canning, 4, Marble Arch, W.

Miscellaneous.

VALVE Lifter for De Dion Motors, does away with compression tap, immediate silence passing horses, grand for coasting, reduces labour in pedalling by one-half; 25s. complete.—Guest, Draycott, Derby.

TWO sets *English Mechanic* cycle motor castings, most difficult work done, owner going in for car; will take £10 for the lot, or sell separately.—No. 1, 944, c/o *The Autocar* Office, Coventry.

VARIABLE Speed Gear Patent for Sale; will give any variation between full speed ahead, stop, reverse, with one movement.—Coombs, Toledo Works, Birmingham.

A REWARD of £10 will be paid to anyone who gives information that will lead to the conviction of the person or persons who removed the platinum tubes from our cars between the 18th and 25th of April.—The British Motor Coupée Co., 366-8, Euston Road, London, N.W.

FRONT SEAT attachment wanted for De Dion tricycle, new or second-hand.—Write only, H., 38, Fairfax Road, South Hampstead, N.W.

SETS of Components for building Chilton's patent new Courier motoret for two persons or parcels delivery, convertible, £12 12s.; send 2s. 6d. for working drawing, credited on first order.—New Courier Cycle Company, Limited, Alexandra St., Wolverhampton.

VALVES, Guest's patent, never require grinding, 10s. each; 1¾ h.p. De Dions increased to 2¼ h.p.; advice given regarding motor troubles; repairs of all kinds executed promptly.—Guest, Engineer, Draycott Mills, Derbyshire.

ONE set of four Benz wheels, second-hand, with solid rubber tyres, backs 36in. diameter, fronts 24 in. diameter, for sale, cheap.—F. Bullock, Strangeways Cycle Works, Bury New Road, Manchester.

PETROL.—Carless, Capel & Leonard, of Hope Chemical Works, and Pharos Works, Hackney Wick, London, N.E., specially distil Petrol, the spirit best adapted for motors, motor carriages, launches, etc., etc. Maximum of efficiency and perfect combustion, therefore great economy and no deposit in cylinders. No smell, no dirt, no trouble. Carless, Capel & Leonard have supplied the above for the Daimler motors for over five years, and hold the highest testimonials. They also supply lubricating oils and greases. Samples and prices on application. Telegrams: Carless, Hackney Wick, Petrol.

Situations Wanted & Vacant.

WANTED, Daimler motor car driver and fitter, thoroughly experienced wheel steerer, for private service.—Apply W. Sewell, 8, Worship Street, London, E.C.

YOUNG Man, aged 20, desires engagement in motor car works, with opportunity of learning. Would not mind cleaning. Willing to be useful.—H. F. 177, Victoria Street, London.

WANTED, place where thorough knowledge of motor cars can be had. No objection to, or amount of, work. Private service would do, if good knowledge could be obtained.—Baron la Costa Lini, c/o R. Mackenzie, 1, Pelham Street, Hastings.

Answers to Correspondents.

NOVICE.—Thanks for information. It is just such happenings as this which do harm, as they go far to substantiate the popular theories as to explosions and conflagrations.

R.A.C.—We have not one of these machines by us at the moment, and cannot call to mind the little handle named, but we will examine one at the first opportunity.

R. A. COBB.—All things being equal you do not require it, but as the compression is usually lower and the speed of rotation and heat of the envelope much less, it is found desirable in practice.

P. B. HUTCHINSON.—Yes, the leather lining should increase the power somewhat, but be sure you have it thoroughly riveted on. It should be white, with just a tinge of yellow, that is, not quite white.

MOTORIST.—The only thing you can do is to have another silencer fitted.

A.R.—Your query is too vague for us to deal with. Do you desire that the ladies should do the driving, or will the ladies be the load only?

Specimen "SMALL ADS" *of the period.*

II
* *The Formative Years* *
1900~1914

98. Tourist Trophy, 1914

THE DEVELOPMENT of the motor car from its first hesitant beginnings to the present day has been astonishingly rapid but never more so than in the years between the beginning of the century and the outbreak of the First World War, years loosely referred to in motoring circles as the Edwardian period. It is for this reason that they have been given the fullest treatment in this book. It was in these years that the car began its swift transformation of our way of life. It began to oust the hansom, the growler and the horse bus from the streets of London and to awaken the roads of the shires to an activity they had not known since the birth of railways. They were roads as yet ill suited to the new vehicles and the problems of the dust menace or the 'dreaded side-slip' were, like police traps, perennial topics for discussion.

Although the car of 1900 was a vast improvement upon its predecessors, it was still in a tentative stage of development and it was not by our standards reliable. That the influence of the horse-drawn carriage still lingered was evident in body styles and the names given to them by coachbuilders. No one could then foresee on what lines the motor car would evolve. Benz still clung obstinately to his slow-speed rear-mounted engine while others favoured a horizontal engine at the front, sometimes mounting the front seats above it. Some still believed that the steam car might ultimately triumph. Yet in five years time orthodox design had been established, while at the end of our short period we see touring cars of recognizably modern form, fitted with electric lighting and starting, quick detachable wheels and other refinements.

The first great advance in design emerged most fittingly from the historic Daimler stable in 1901. After Gottlieb Daimler died in 1900, his partner Wilhelm Maybach carried on the business and designed and built for a wealthy client named Emile Jellinek a special car. It went into production under the name of Jellinek's daughter, a name to conjure with in the motoring world henceforth—Mercedes. This car presented for the first time many features which would eventually be universally adopted: a pressed-steel chassis frame, a handsome honeycomb radiator instead of a serpentine coil of gilled tubing, a 35 h.p. four-cylinder engine with magneto ignition and all valves mechanically operated, a plate clutch and a gearbox with 'gate' change.

In the luxury touring-car class the Mercedes had no rival until 1906/7 when there appeared the prototype of the famous Rolls-Royce 'Silver Ghost' which set a standard of refinement, of smoothness and silence and fine craftsmanship which has never been surpassed. Thus, in the Rolls-Royce and in other fine cars such as the Napier, the Daimler and the Lanchester, the British motor industry showed that in six years it had more than overcome its initial handicap. Each year new makes appeared to swell the ranks of British cars. Many of their names are forgotten now, but others such as Wolseley, Vauxhall, Sunbeam, Talbot, Austin and Rover would become household words. With the adoption of pressed-steel frame members, chassis became longer and lower and the old rear entrance 'tonneau' body in which the rear passengers were perched well behind the back axle gave place to the longer 'side entrance' body within the wheelbase. Thus the orthodox open touring car, known when it first appeared as a 'torpedo', was evolved. All the famous makers mentioned above produced medium-powered cars of this type and one of them, in the 'Prince Henry' type Vauxhall 'fast touring car', built the ancestor of the sports cars which would appear in the 1920s.

Although the best 'torpedo' touring cars were handsome vehicles, closed coachwork continued to be, with rare exceptions, high, angular and ugly. It was in this department that the craftsman carriage builder clung most tenaciously to traditional ideas. His bodies were magnificently built but they were appallingly heavy and made only grudging concessions to the new line which longer and lower chassis demanded.

Until 1910 the average 'light car' or *voiturette* had a single- or twin-cylinder engine and appeared in a variety of weird and wonderful forms. It was seldom a desirable form of transport though the type survived into the 1920s in the form of the cyclecar. But in 1910 another milestone of design appeared in the guise of the litt'e type 13 Bugatti. This was a large car in exquisite miniature and the ancestor of all the light cars of the post-war years. By 1914 many of them had already appeared on English roads: Calcott, Singer, Crouch, Standard, Swift, A.C., and—most significant of all—the Morris Oxford.

A significant transatlantic product was the famous 'Model T' Ford, the first mass-produced car, a full-sized car of great reliability selling at a price which rivalled that of the crudest British light car.

On the Continent the great road races continued to be the supreme testing ground and British manufacturers suffered to some extent from the fact that road racing in this country was illegal. Yet the loss was not so great as it might have been for in the first years of the century when the French Panhards, Mors and De Dietrich were invincible the conception of a racing car consisted of cramming the largest possible engine into the lightest possible chassis. Little attempt was made to improve engine efficiency and the influence of such machines on production car design was limited. The tragedies of the Paris-Madrid race of 1903 brought to an end the great series of trans-continental road races and, after the last event in the Gordon Bennett series in 1905, the French Grand Prix became the *grande epreuve*. In the following year Brooklands Track was completed to the immense benefit of our motor industry. At this time, too, the age of giants was drawing to its close. Mercedes from Germany and Fiat from Italy had successfully challenged French supremacy in Grand Prix racing, but in 1912 Georges Boillot not only redeemed the honour of France but, by defeating the 'giant racers' with a Peugeot of only $7\frac{1}{2}$ litres capacity, showed that henceforth success in motor racing would be a question of brains rather than brawn. The successful road racing car in the years 1912 to 1914 became the embodiment of all that was most advanced in automobile design. With high-efficiency overhead camshaft engine, improved chassis design, four-wheel brakes and quick-detachable wheels it foreshadowed, on the eve of the First World War, the best in production-car design during the 1920s. If we consider the Rolls-Royce or the typical Grand Prix car of 1914 and contrast them with the Panhard et Levassor of 1900 we can appreciate that these were indeed the great formative years.

ACTS OF VIOLATION.

AS WE ARE SELLING

De=Dion=Bouton Voiturettes

for £190,

and guarantee delivery within four weeks of order, our competitors have thought fit to attempt to induce purchasers from buying cars from us.

We will GUARANTEE our customers, and ACCEPT TO DEFEND any action or actions that may possibly—but not probably—be taken against them and to refund them any costs or damages that may be incurred.

If our competitors really desire to show their justification of their attempts to prevent persons buying from us, THEY WOULD SERVE US WITH A WRIT FOR INFRINGEMENT OF PATENTS, AND WE SHOULD BE PLEASED TO ACCEPT SUCH.

In the meantime WE APPEAL to the public to UPHOLD US by giving us their custom and accepting our guarantee, as we DESIRE for the BENEFIT OF THE MOTORING PUBLIC at large to either MAINTAIN an OPEN MARKET or to have definite PROOFS of the VALIDITY OF ALLEGED PATENTS, and whether there is a JUSTIFICATION in demanding LICENSE PLATES to be affixed to cars at an EXORBITANT PRICE.

WE GUARANTEE ALL OUR CARS.

AUTOMOBILE ASSOCIATION, LTD.,

HOLLAND PARK AVENUE, LONDON, W.

99/102. In Britain the new century opened inauspiciously with a shouting match in the advertising columns of the motoring press as, by threat and bluster, H. J. Lawson endeavoured unsuccessfully to uphold his British Motor Company's claim to a monopoly of master patents. In America, George B. Selden tried the same tactics with more success until he was finally defeated by Henry Ford. The new industry was far too virile to be strangled at birth in such a fashion.

❧ ❧ ❧ Warning. ❧ ❧ ❧

We beg to caution intending purchasers against certain unauthorised dealers and manufacturers **who are trying to palm off IMITATIONS of our Motors as genuine,** and we emphatically state that we have given **no license** to make our cars in England.

Messrs. HEWETSON Ltd., of Dean Street, Soho, London,

are our sole representatives for Great Britain, and only Benz Cars sold through this firm or their agents will come under our guarantee. We shall not supply any parts or replacements to persons obtaining here and there one of our cars indirectly.

The ORIGINAL BENZ Car is always the best.

It is the result of fifteen years' study and experience, and, since its invention in 1885, the first car in the world. Unscrupulous people copy our work, but

The ORIGINAL BENZ Car has never been surpassed.

We strongly recommend anyone, before buying a motor car, to carefully read the results of the Automobile Club trials last summer, and compare the performance of our cars with that of other makers. **WE WISH FOR NO BETTER ADVERTISEMENT.** This can be obtained from Messrs. HEWETSON's at cost price, 1/3, post free.

We particularly caution purchasers of Benz Cars against parting with **ANY MONEY WHATEVER,** either as payment on account or deposit, **UNTIL THEIR CAR IS READY FOR THEM TO TAKE AWAY.**

BENZ & CO., Rheinische Gasmotorenfabrik A.G.,

MANNHEIM.

Established in 1883.

103. Dr F. W. Lanchester, who built his first car so early as 1895, was responsible for the first entirely original British design to be built commercially. Concerned to reduce engine vibration, he designed an air-cooled flat-twin engine with two crankshafts rotating in opposite directions. In this picture Mr and Mrs Lanchester Senior are seen in their 10 h.p. front-entrance phaeton.

104. The Earl of Dudley's Panhard et Levassor at Elmley Lovett, 1902. Except that the front seat squab is unusually high, this is a typical example of the early Edwardian touring car with its gilled-tube radiator and rear-entrance tonneau body built out, clover-leaf fashion, over the rear mudguards.

105. Prototype: the famous 1901 Mercedes with honeycomb radiator, gate change and pressed steel chassis frame.

106. Visitors to the 1903 Gordon Bennett race in Ireland, a study in back views not remarkable for beauty. Notice that one car carries a continental registration number while two have spare tyres tied behind.

107. Mrs Lloyd's 30 h.p. Daimler at Brighton Speed Trials, 1905. As chassis became longer the side entrance tonneau body began to supersede the older types. The car still has chain drive and lacks screen or hood, but the famous Daimler radiator has already arrived.

108. 1905 six-cylinder Napier. The famous firm of D. Napier & Sons of Lambeth were among the pioneers of the British motor industry and the first to build a 'six' commercially (in 1904). The side-entrance body is notably longer and lower than that of the Daimler above.

The enjoyment of life is dependent on time, space, money—the

OLDSMOBILE

lengthens out yet economizes all three. It is a demonstrated public utility—as indispensable as the telephone, the typewriter or the sewing machine. It fits into the every day requirements of the business and professional man. It takes the "waits" out of life.

A price available to the average pocketbook, low cost of maintenance, simplicity of construction, and easy control, are Oldsmobile characteristics. Point for point, the Oldsmobile shows the most advanced improvements in automobile building; the side springs are a revelation in spring suspension; brakes are always dependable in time of emergency; horse power equipment easily equal to any demand. Cars that can stand the work of a transcontinental race like the one now in progress between the two Oldsmobile 7 h. p. runabouts, Old Steady and Old Scout, are a pretty safe investment for every day use.

Note the range of prices:

Standard Runabout, 7 h. p., . .	$650	Touring Car, 20 h. p., . . .	$1,400
Touring Runabout, 7 h. p., . .	$750	Delivery Car, 16 h. p., . . .	$2,000
	Ten Passenger Wagonette, $2,200		

All prices f. o. b. factory. Our handsome new catalog "A" free on request. Send 10 cents for six months' trial subscription to Motor Talk, a magazine devoted to automobile interests.

Olds Motor Works, Detroit, U. S. A.

Member A. L. A. M.

Drawing by T. Dart Walker.
Copyrighted 1905, Brownell & Humphrey, Detroit.

109. As this advertisement of 1905 shows, the 'horseless carriage' (in the form of the buggy) lingered longest in America. There is nothing out of date about the advertising copy, however. To satisfy English taste, the Oldsmobile sold over here was fitted with a dummy bonnet which held luggage.

110. Frederick Eastmead, 16/20 Sunbeam, 1907. In this typical medium-powered, high-quality Edwardian of the middle period the orthodox touring car lines are beginning to emerge. The seats no longer project so far above the body line while the car is equipped with hood and windscreen.

111. This 1907 Adams was one of the few cars other than the Ford to use the epicyclic gear principle which was later to be embodied in the self-change gearbox. This was how one got at the formidable-looking works. Failure to secure the body after making a repair could have interesting consequences.

112. The arrival of the immortal 'Silver Ghost' Rolls-Royce in 1907 was one of the greatest landmarks in motoring history. In this 1907 group outside the 'Cat & Fiddle', Buxton, four cars are being demonstrated to pressmen. The drivers, from the left, are: Claude Johnson (in the original Silver Ghost), Hon. C. S. Rolls, Percy Northey, and Wright, the works manager.

113. *Above:* This Simms car of 1907 is fitted with the pneumatic rubber safety bumper which F. R. Sims patented in this year. It was years ahead of its time.

114. Chains are disappearing; this 1910 Daimler was the first of this make to be fitted with a live axle. Note also the spare rim and tyre and the way in which, before the days of wipers, the 'cape cart' hood was extended well forward with the object of keeping rain off the upper part of the screen.

115/116. Whereas the magnificent 1910 Rolls-Royce has that curvilinear opulence of the true Edwardian tradition, the 1911 Vauxhall (*right*) shows the new 'torpedo' line beginning to emerge. The scuttle is no longer vertical but curved up from the bonnet while the seat backs are about to disappear within the high straight-sided body.

117. 1913, the Mercedes Torpedo. The Touring car has now reached a point in its evolution where it would remain without radical change in appearance for the next twenty years. Notice the unbroken line from radiator cap to windscreen and the seats well within the body. Note too, that Mercedes still cling to chain drive.

118. This 1914 30 h.p. Sheffield Simplex shows three further refinements: electric headlamps, Rudge-type detachable wire wheels and the new domed mudguards which soften the severity of the straighter lines and break the last link with horse-carriage tradition.

119-120. British and Continental forerunners of the vintage sports cars of the '20s, both of 1914. Right: The 'Prince Henry' Vauxhall. Below: A Peugeot with special *Labourdette* body.

121/22. This Straker Squire is typical of the open two/three seater which became popular towards the end of our period. The dickey seat passenger, however, was mercilessly exposed to the elements.

123. Compared with th smooth lines of the bes European cars, the famou 'Model T' Ford looks dis concertingly angular. But was the world's first mass produced motor car, at onc absurdly cheap and ex tremely reliable, thus earnin world-wide popularity.

124. As the epitome of late-Edwardian elegance this 'Edinburgh' Rolls-Royce makes an appropriate tailpiece to this section. Note the additio windscreen for the protection of the rear passengers.

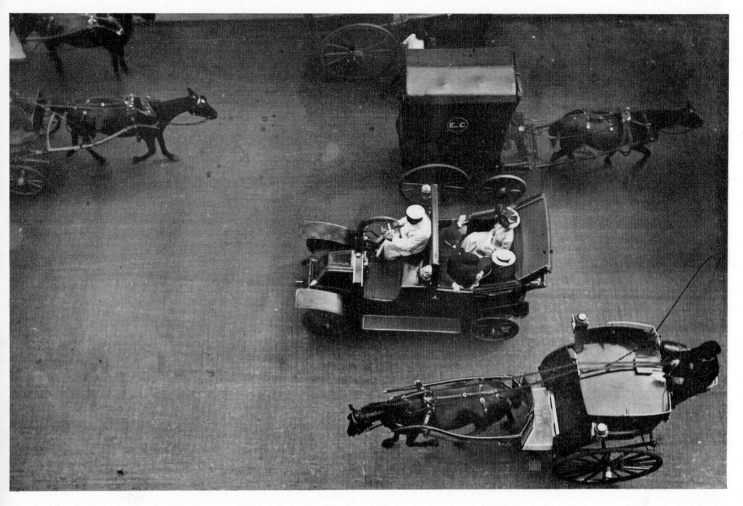

125. The new between the old in a London street seen from an unusual angle.

126. At the beginning of the century closed cars were few and far between. Here is one of the exceptions, closed coachwork on a Tour de France-type Bollee chassis.

127. London taxicabs, *circa* 1906

128-131. In Edwardian London the horse-drawn vehicle for long retained its place as *the* fashionable town carriage. Hence, in its fight to win acceptance in this field, the motor car emulated the electric brougham by trying to conceal its vulgar 'works'. Here are the Straker McConnell, the eight-cylinder Rolls-Royce 'legal limit' (Yes, even this Homer nodded), and, below, the Argyll and the extraordinary Vauxhall hansom. All of 1906 vintage.

132. The two-seater coupe was a rarity in 1906. This example, boasting a very early dickey seat, is on an Arrol Johnston chassis.

133. The Coupe de Ville, with its blue-glassed carriage lamps and its basket work lower panels, was the height of elegance and the only example of the horse-carriage tradition to survive down to our own day.

134. 1906 Daimler Landaulette. The builders of town carriages soon sensibly abandoned the horseless carriage conception but, like the coachman on his box, they exposed the unfortunate chauffeur to all the fury of the elements.

135-136. Both this Richard Brasier (left) and the Napier show the driver more mercy. Both have windscreens while the former has a fixed roof and the latter a roll-down hood.

137. Compared with the contemporary tourer, the town carriage of 1914 still looks somewhat angular and archaic to us. Yet a car such as this 45 h.p. sleeve valve Daimler was superbly silent and comfortable. The adoption, after much experiment, of the Knight sleeve valve by Daimler in 1909 caused quite a furore. Some predicted failure, others that the poppet valve would soon become extinct. Daimler did not finally abandon sleeve valves until 1936.

138. This 45 h.p. Napier Pullman Limousine of 1914 represents the last pre-war word in fully-enclosed cars. Note such advanced details as the 'Vee' windscreen and the side lamps.

139. Although it looks ugly to us, this burnished aluminium Gladiator caused a sensation in 1914 and in its revolutionary breakaway from the severe rectangular form which dominated all closed coachwork at this time forecast the shape of things to come.

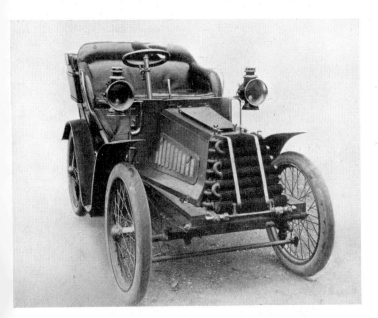

140-143. At the beginning of the century the *voiturette*, as it was then called, was a stark machine bearing little resemblance to the large car and usually powered by a single-cylinder engine. Above: 1900 Humber (left) and the 5 h.p. Decauville. Right: The 1903 5 h.p. Vauxhall, first of the marque.

144/145. By 1906 the *voiturette*, though still a 'one lunger', had begun to look more like a motor car. On the left is a 6 h.p. Rover and on the right a 6 h.p. Calthorpe with a hood whose only virtue would seem to be to avert sun-stroke.

146. This Turner car illustrates the orthodox light car form in process of evolution. Note the acetylene generator for the headlamps on the running board.

147. A demonstration of cyclecars in 1912. The horse is visibly outraged.

148-149. Forerunners: Above: Quantity and Quality, Model T Ford and Type 13 Bugatti. Designed by Ettore Bugatti in 1911 the Type 13 was not a crude runabout but a superbly-built luxury car in miniature with a fine performance. Like its many successors, some of which appear in the following pages, it was a true 'light car'. Below: Another outstanding achievement was the diminutive Baby Peugeot which, with its toy-like four-cylinder engine anticipated the Austin 'Seven' and other 'babies' by many years.

150-154. The parting of the ways. When the true light car appeared the cruder and simpler tradition of the early *voiturettes* was perpetuated by the cyclecar which continued to serve the impecunious motorist until the Austin Seven consigned it to limbo. Top: The G.N. was by far the most successful of true cyclecars. Here is a muster of early belt-driven models at Petersfield after a hill-climb at South Harting. In circle: the Wall Tricar. Right: the Buckingham with long belt drive and exposed magneto promises lots of trouble. Bottom: two A.C. sociables with A.C. cars and a Chater Lea.

155-158. Light cars of 1914. Top: Three-seater Meteorite. Right: The aptly-named Crouch. Left: A.C. fixed-head and Standard drop-head coupés.

159-162. Light cars of 1914. Top: The Swift. Left: The Humberette. Centre Right: The Stellite, ancestor of the Wolseley Ten. Below: the G.W.K. with friction drive.

63/164. Light cars of 1914. The Singer (top) and—last and most significant of all—the Morris Oxford, whose 'bull nose' radiator would soon become as famous and familiar as the more angular profile of the 'Model T'.

165. One of the first cars to standardize independent front-wheel suspension, using a transverse leaf spring, was the Sizaire et Naudin single-cylinder *voiturette*. Here Messieurs Sizaire (left) and Naudin conduct their machines on the Paris 'Velodrome'.

166-167. First to standardize independent suspension in England, using coil springs, was Morgan on the famous three-wheeler which bore his name. He is seen (left) after winning the hour cyclecar race at Brooklands in 1912. The Baby C.I.D. (right) also used independent suspension.

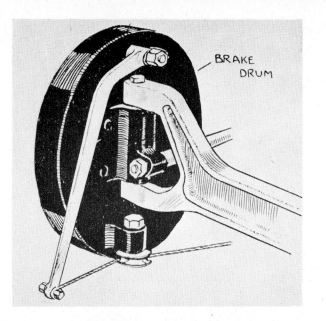

BRAKE DRUM

168-171. Few people associate front wheel brakes with the Edwardian era. Several manufacturers introduced them, though with small success, and although racing cars were using them in 1914 it was not until after the war that they were widely employed. Top left: Bowden brake fitted to a Mercedes in 1906. Right: Thames car brake of 1909. Below, left and right: Crossley and Sheffield Simplex.

172. Electrics: the belt-driven dynamo and starter motor on the Arrol Johnston 1914 model.

173-174. Under the bonnets of the 1906 Clement Talbot and 1914 16 h.p. Darracq. Compared with the primitive and untidy machinery of the earlier cars, the average car engine of 1914 was a beautifully clean and highly finished unit.

175. The White & Poppe engine of the 1914 Morris Oxford. Notice the unit construction of engine and gearbox, a practice destined to become universal.

176. The majority of manufacturers used side-val engines. Although overhead valves were widely adopte in racing cars, they considered that improved performan would not justify the complication and, they thoug unreliability. Ettore Bugatti, however, was one of t notable exceptions and this picture shows the overhea camshaft unit of his Type 13. Note especially the we designed exhaust manifold and contrast it with t restricted internal manifold of the Darracq.

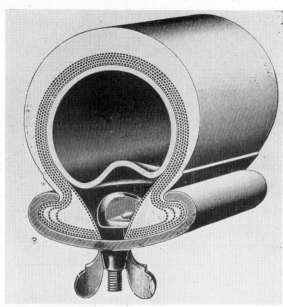

177-178. Tyres were the greatest bugbear of the Edwardian motorist and road races were tyre massacres. This is a scene behind the pits at the Coupe des Voiturettes at Boulogne, 1910. Tyre changing was a grim business, for not only were the early wheels non-detachable but the beaded edge covers were held in their rims by a number of 'security bolts' as shown on right.

179. Security bolts notwithstanding, tyres not infrequently flew off the wheels to the embarrassment of the driver. This gentleman, however, presses on regardless.

180. The joys of roadside puncture mending.

181-183. The Stepney spare wheel which could be attached to a punctured road wheel was a clumsy expedient which preceded the detachable wheel. Below: Michelin and Dunlop lightened the motorist's burden when they produced their detachable rims. This is the Dunlop rim and on the right stands the man whose bearded face became a trade mark—J. B. Dunlop.

184. The detachable wheel took the dread out of punctures. Note the metal-studded tyre which was so popular in this period.

185. The tyres themselves improved. This Lanchester is fitted with the new Palmer cord tyres which had a much-improved type of fabric casing that made practicable tyres of more generous section. The wheel discs are another innovation.

186-187. London in 1910. Although cars predominate in this view of Piccadilly, many of the well-to-do remained faithful to their carriages as is revealed by the scene outside the Royal Academy on private view day.

188-189. Although these views of Trafalgar Square and Hyde Park Corner fill us with envy to-day, they were originally captioned 'congested traffic dangers'.

190/191. By 1912 cars were appearing in numbers at public events. Above: Derby Day. Below: The review of the fleet at Spithead.

192/194. If his propeller shaft disintegrated, if he had an argument with a tram or ran out of petrol, the Edwardian motorist had to cope with the situation as best he could unless a good Samaritan came along.

195. Garages such as this were few and far between and had no breakdown equipment.

196. A tense moment: on the muddy roads 'the dreaded side slip' was the frequent result of over-exuberance.

197. In dry weather the mud turned to flour-like dust which the passing of a car raised in clouds. Designers at first tried to overcmoe this on the car itself. Here is a competitor in the anti-dust trials held by the R.A.C. at Brooklands in 1908.

198-199. Methods of road repair were often crude in the extreme and the unfortunate motorist would be suddenly confronted by a sea of mud or by a tyre-destroying layer of loose stones as in this scene at Nailsworth.

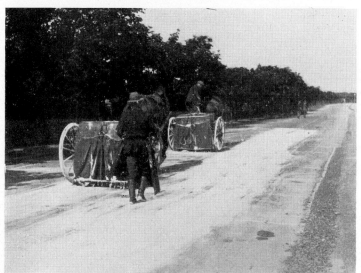

200-205. Various primitive attempts were made to improve road surfaces and lay dust. By sweeping, by water carts and by spreading calcium. But it was soon realized that the answer lay in the use of tar or bitumen products. Centre Right: An early tar spreader is pictured at the important dust laying experiments at Staines in May 1907. Bottom: On the eve of the war experiments were being made with concrete roads, while the opening of Brighton's new tarmac road in 1910 called for a procession of flag-bedecked cars.

Motor Notes

By "PETROL"

As January 1, 1904, gets nearer and nearer, motorists will have to consider the new Act which comes into force on that date, and the effect of such Act. Every owner of a motor-car will have to—

(1) Take out a licence for his car	£2	2	0
(2) Register his car with the County Council, and obtain a number for it	1	0	0
(3) Take out a licence to drive		5	0
(4) Take out a licence for his driver		5	0
(5) Take out a licence to keep a male servant		15	0
	£4	7	0

Now the first step the Local Government Board has taken is to draft proposals for the consideration of the Councils, and like some —indeed, all—of the provisions of the new Act, many of their suggestions are absurd. I have many times urged that we should take our information from France, where legislation with regard to automobiles is far ahead of us, and I again urge it. Take the size of the number plates as suggested by the Local Government Board. Anyone who has ever looked at a car—it may be with aversion—must know that many of them will be unable to affix the plates to the front of their cars without either dragging them along the road, perching them on a bracket on high, or preventing the proper action of the radiator. I give below an illustration of the plate (to scale) proposed for England and that used abroad, although I know of no regulation there giving such exact details as are required by our authorities.

11in. by 10in.
SUGGESTED PLATE FOR UNITED KINGDOM

17in. by 5in.
PLATE AS USED ABROAD

THE PENALTIES

It is invidious and unpatriotic to compare our legislation with that of foreign countries, but it is certainly necessary on this question. Why are there no police traps except in England? If this most un-British custom is continued under the new Act, what will be the result? Practically the extermination of motoring; and I am afraid many people will rejoice. But the intention of our Legislature was not to kill, but to control. After January 1, it will be possible for a policeman to take note of your number, and a summons will follow in due course, without your being aware of having committed any offence against the law, as it is quite impossible to estimate speed, say, between nineteen and twenty-one miles an hour; and there is no question that the police nowadays swear to anything in a motor case. Only last week I was summoned (for the first time I am glad to say, although I have driven many thousands of miles in England and abroad), and the constable deliberately swore, after "kissing the book," to quite a different number of seconds to that given me on the day in question. As a matter of fact, he reduced the time in my favour, but it showed great inaccuracy. This is a frequent occurrence now, and I dread to think what will occur when you have not even the knowledge that you have committed an offence. That vindictiveness is shown is evident from the fact that, although the magistrates know twenty miles will be the limit in a month or two, they daily fine unfortunate motorists £5 for going eighteen miles an hour.

207-210. Friends and Foes. The Edwardian motorist also faced the legal hazards of hostile police. The two top pictures are from a 1909 series satirizing the methods used for timing cars in police traps, the top picture being captioned 'the Sundial method'. But the motorist had friends too. On left is a Motor Union patrol of 1907 and (right) an A.A. scout of 1909.

211/213. Mr Stenson Cooke of the A.A. receives a report from a patrol. Right: The A.A. scout warned members of police traps by standing to attention instead of saluting. Bottom: You needed good eyesight to spot this early A.A. route sign mounted on an Inn signpost at Merstham.

4/215. An early ancestor of the modern 'radio cop' and a typically discouraging signpost of the period.

216/217. Following the precedent of the great 1,000 miles trial of 1900, trials and hill-climbs became increasingly popular throughout our period. Here and in the pages which follow are a few glimpses of these events. Above: Competitors starting on the Glenshee hillclimb, Scottish trial, June 1905. Below: Competitors at Inverary, Scottish trials, 1906.

218. The Rolls-Royce 30 h.p. six-cylinder on the Devil's Elbow, Scottish trials, 1906.

219. American challengers: two Cadillacs weigh in for the Irish A.C. trials, 1907.

220. 'They wept like anything to see. . . .' ed Straight and A. Ebblewhite of Brook- nds' fame, timekeeping on Magilligan rand, Irish Trials, 1907.

221. '. . . such quantities of sand.' H. P. Wilson (18/24 Austin) makes his run on Magilligan Strand.

222. 'All together . . . heave!' If a co[m]petitor ran out of the road there was [a] breakdown crane to help. Irish Tria[ls] 1908.

223. The lunch stop at Limerick, Irish Trials, 1908.

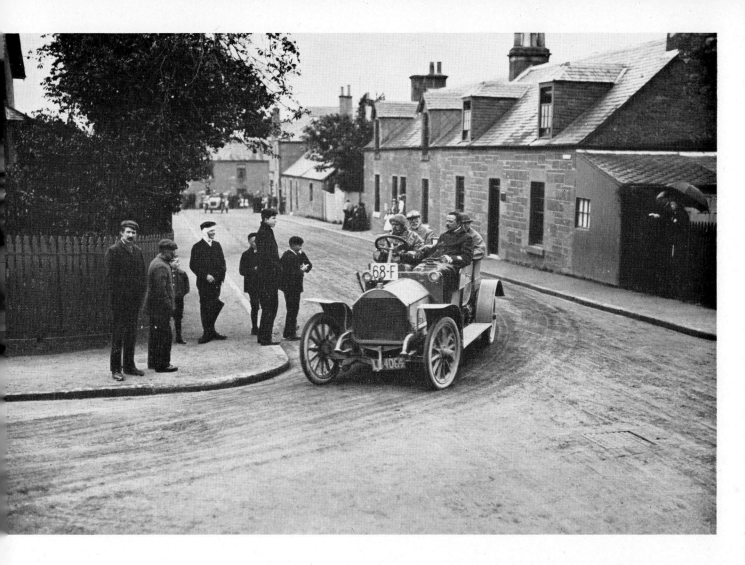

224/226. The great 2,000 miles trial of the R.A.C. in 1908 was an outstanding event of the era and was distinguished by the performance of the new Vauxhall and Talbot cars.
Above: Coming into Blairgowrie. Below, left: The lunch stop at Blairgowrie. Below, right: On the bend of Cairnomount.

227. Ballinslaughter hill climb, Irish Trials, 1908.

228. Stanley Webb's Ford comes into secret check at Stilton, Essex Club twenty-four hour trial, August 1910.

229. Cars celebrating the tenth anniversary of the first 1,000 miles trial at the Eleanor Cross, Northampton. At the head of the procession, Lord Montagu's 'Silver Ghost' carries the original flag borne in 1900.

30. 'Will she make it?' An anxious moment for the Morgan on Jailsworth Ladder, 1914.

231. Night Trial: Prevost's Morris starts from Highgate on the M.C.C. London-Edinburgh, May 1914.

232. All sizes and shapes: Competitors in the Cyclecar Club's trial of February 1914 assemble in the paddock at Brooklands.

233/234. Ironbridge Hill-climb, 1910. Louis Coatelen, Sunbeam, at the start and Hancock's Vauxhall on the hairpin bend.

235. An early encounter at South Harti Coleman, White Steamer, before the st of a challenge match with Miss Levi Napier. In sprint events steam was still formidable opponent and Coleman w his match.

6/237. Shelsley Walsh, one of the first and most famous of all hill climbs. Bird, Sunbeam, leaving the start and Lomax, Vauxhall, coming out the 'S' bend.

238. Caerphilly, June 1913. Day doing some spectacular cornering with his 25 Talbot.

239/240. The year 1913 saw the appearance, in the hands of J. Higginson, of a special Vauxhall developed from the already famous 'Prince Henry' model. This was none other than the prototype of the immortal '30/98'. Higginson is here seen on Beacon Hill, while on right the car is standing in the paddock at Pateley Bridge.

241-242. Aston Hill, 1914. W. O. Bentley finishing in his D.F.P. Right: A Bugatti takes the first bend.

43-244. South Harting, 1914. Left: A lady with a very small Mathis attached to a very large steering wheel preparing to start. Right: Leno in Baby Peugeot passes a wrecked Carden which had overturned on Chalk Pit corner.

245. The Edwardian Era may truly be called the heroic age of motor racing when the men whose names have become legendary—de Knyff, Jenatzy, Farman, Girardot, Gabriel, Jarrott to name only a few—thundered down the continental roads in their 'giant racers'. The engines of these monsters became steadily larger and chassis proportionately flimsier until 1912 when a new conception of the racing car emerged. The following pages present a few memories of those far-off, dramatic days. The picture above shows de Haenen's contemporary drawing of S. F. Edge during his famous twenty-four hour record run on the newly opened Brooklands Track in the six-cylinder Napier. Driving single-handed throughout and averaging over 65 m.p.h., many regarded Edge's performance as the greatest British motoring achievement of the period.

246-249. Land speed record holders. Top: First to achieve 100 m.p.h. on the road; Arthur Duray in the 110 h.p. four-cylinder opposed-piston Gobron-Brillié. In the hands of Duray and Rigolly the car raised the flying kilo record from 84.21 m.p.h. in 1903 to 103.56 m.p.h. in 1904. Next; in December 1905 at Arles, Hemery put the record up to 109.65 m.p.h. in this 200 h.p. 'vee' eight-cylinder Darracq. Our next picture shows Fred Marriott in the astonishing Stanley steam car 'The Rocket'. At Ormond Beach in January 1906 the Stanley captured the flying kilo at 121.57 m.p.h. and the mile at 127.66 m.p.h. Later the car achieved a much higher speed before it crashed into the sea and the Stanley brothers forbade any further attempts. Bottom: The last successful attempt before the war and the first

[Continued below

nder the 'mean of two runs in both directions' ruling, as made by Hornsted in a 200 h.p. Benz using the ilway straight at Brooklands. Here two unsung heroes deavour to urge the monster into life for its first run. he Benz raised the kilo record to 124.1 m.p.h. with a st run at 128.16 m.p.h.

250. Victors of the great trans-continental road races: Fournier, 60 h.p. Mors at Bordeaux after winning the Paris-Bordeaux race of 1901. Average speed: 53.0 m.p.h.

251. Henri Farman in his 70 h.p Panhard at Vienna after winning the Paris-Vienna Race of 1902. This course was extremely severe and the winner's average for the 615 mile was 38.4 m.p.h.

252. S. F. Edge and Montague Napier in the four-cylinder Napier which won the Gordon Bennett cup in 1902. This trophy was for competition between teams of three cars selected by each country. France, undisputed masters of the sport at this time did not take the cup seriously and in this year it was run concurrently with the Paris-Vienna to a finish at Salzburg. But the French nominees met with misfortune and their compatriots were shocked to discover that Edge though an 'also ran' in the Vienna race, had won the Gordon Bennett.

253. Premonition? A strangely rapt Lorraine Barrow awaits his turn to start from Paris on his last race. He was mortally injured when his de Dietrich struck a tree after a dog had jammed the steering gear.

254. The intrepid Madame du Gast in her Paris-Madrid de Dietrich. The only woman driver in this and other early motoring events, Madame stopped to give first aid to a crashed driver, then pressed on undaunted, being the forty-fifth car to finish.

255-256. Louis Renault put up a magnificent performance in his 30 h.p. Renault averaging 62.3 m.p.h. from Paris to Bordeaux to win the light car class and come second on general classification. As Louis thundered down the long white straights he did not know that his brother Marcel, driving a sister car, had crashed fatally near Ruffec while trying to pass Thèry.

257. It seemed as though all the misfortunes which *could* have befallen in earlier events happened in this one race. The road to Bordeaux was littered with wrecked cars and the race was stopped at this, the first day's stage. Here is the outright winner, Gabriel, o h.p. Mors, finishing at Bordeaux. Starting 68th, he drove through the dust clouds, the wrecks and the uncontrolled crowds to average 65.3 m.p.h. for the 342 miles, one of the outstanding feats in motoring history.

258-260. As a result of Edge's lucky win, the Gordon Bennett race was taken much more seriously and the 1903 event, staged in Ireland because of the British victory, aroused immense interest. Here (left) are two '70' Panhards in charge of de Knyff and Farman with a spare car, while Jarrott and Stocks in their Napiers are seen below. Above: While European racing cars conformed to a pattern, American designers were much more original, if less successful. Thus Winton's Winton Special had a horizontal straight-eight engine slung amidships. This is how Winton and his mechanic occupied themselves for much of the race.

261. In the event the honour of France was not restored neither could Britain successfully defend the cup. It went to **Germany**. Here the winner Camille Jenatzy, the famous 'Red Devil', leans from his Mercedes to receive congratulations.

262. The supreme Panhard; it is 1904 and Heath has just won the Circuit des Ardennes race for Panhard for the third year in succession. But new names were appearing in the list and the day of this most successful of early racing cars was almost done.

263. Famous British driver: Charles Jarrott and his mechanic Bianchi in the Wolseley 'Beetle' which he drove in the 1904 Gordon Bennett at Homburg. He finished twelfth while Thèry (Richard Brasier) at last restored the cup to France.

264. The last Gordon Bennett race, in 1905, was held on a tortuous circuit in the Auvergne and was again won by Thèry, here seen during the French eliminating trials.

265. The winner, Duray, de Dietrich at speed in the 1906 Circuit des Ardennes.

266. With the passing of the Gordon Bennett contest, British interests centred on the series of Tourist Trophy races held in the Isle of Man. Here one of the Vauxhalls is being drawn by a horse to the start of the first of these races in 1905. It was won by an Arrol Johnston.

267. In the 1906 T.T. the Hon. C. S. Rolls scored an impressive win with a Rolls-Royce 'Light Twenty'.

268. Like the side-car occupants in modern motorcycle racing, the passengers in the T.T. cars performed perilous acrobatic feats on the corners.

269. The elaborate regulations for the 1907 T.T. prescribed a large frontal area. Hence the wooden screen on this 25 h.p. Gladiator.

270. Victory for a British driver: Moore Brabazon (now Lord Brabazon of Tara) takes Bastogne corner on the Minerva with which he won the race for Kaiserpriez cars on the Ardennes Circuit in 1907.

271/272. The Pekin to Paris contest of 1907 could scarcely be called a race, but it was a feat of endurance without parallel in motoring annals. Here is the winner, Prince Borghese, and on the right he is seen arriving in Paris in his Italia.

273. In 1906, the Hon. C. S. Rolls made a record run from Monte Carlo to London in the T.T. winning Rolls-Royce. Here he is with Massac Buist beside him and Swindley of *The Autocar* on the pavement.

274. Another fantastic 'race' of this period was the New York to Paris of 1908. Here the winner, Montague Roberts in the American 60 h.p. Thomas Flyer, is seen on the first stage from New York to Buffalo.

275. Trumpeter, what are you sounding now? Before the days of public address systems in continental road racing, trumpeters warned the stands and pits of the approach of a car. On the long circuits the cars soon became well strung out.

276. Goux, two-cylinder (80 × 280 mm.) Peugeot, Boulogne, 1910. By limiting total piston area, Edwardian *voiturette* racing produced freak machines with a phenomenal stroke/bore ratio. Yet they went very quickly.

277. The American classic at this time was the Vanderbilt Cup which attracted all the best European drivers. Here is Hemery (Darracq) winning the 1905 race.

278. A dramatic moment in the 1906 Vanderbilt: the mechanic of Duray's de Dietrich nearly falls out in his efforts to rescue a spare tyre and rim which has come adrift, but is hauled back by Duray. The winner was Wagner (Darracq) with Duray third.

279. Perhaps the greatest American driver of the day was Joe Tracy, seen here in the Royal Tourist which he drove in the 1904 Vanderbilt. The following year, after working all night to replace a cracked cylinder, he drove the American No. 7 Locomobile into third place against the finest continental opposition.

280. The first supercharged car in the world: the 1908 six-cylinder blown Chadwick. In the 1908 Vanderbilt the car was in the lead on the sixth lap (out of eleven) when magneto trouble beset it. It was successful at Giant's Despair and other American events. The 'power bulge' in the bonnet side betrays the supercharger which was a three-stage centrifugal type belt driven from the flywheel at 20,000 r.p.m. It compressed air only.

281. The ban on any form of racing on the public road in Britain (a special Act had to be passed before the 1903 Gordon Bennett could be held in Ireland) was a serious handicap to the development of the British motor industry. It was in 1906 that Mr H. F. Locke-King decided to remedy matters, very largely at his own risk by building, at Brooklands near Weybridge, the first motor track of its kind in the world. Here it is under construction in 1906.

282-285. Scenes at the opening of the track and the first meeting, 1907. Lord Lonsdale arrives in his Mercedes; the procession of cars from the paddock; the start of a race, most of the earliest competitors drove stripped touring cars. The first casualty: Herman, driving Moore Brabazon' Minerva, overturned on the Members' banking at the September meeting.

286. Motoring personalities in the paddock. Left to right: Hutton, Napier, Edge, Orde, Lord Lonsdale, Lord Montague and Rodakowski, first clerk of the course.

288. Brooklands very soon stimulated British designers. Here, in 1909, is A. J. Hancock in the single-seater Vauxhall 'KN', one of the first cars to be fully streamlined and the first 3 litre to achieve 100 m.p.h.

287 and 289. Brooklands was the nurse of driving talent also. Here are two of her first and most celebrated sons, Dario Resta (top) and Kenelm Lee Guinness.

290-291. As a result of Brooklands, British cars and drivers soon bulked large in the International record book. Perhaps the most notable pre-war achievement (aside from Edge's twenty-four hour run) was that of Percy Lambert in his 25 h.p. Talbot in 1912. By raising the world's hour record to 103.84 m.p.h., he became the first man to cover 100 miles in the hour. After his tragic death in a later record attempt a plaque was placed on the Club-house wall.

292. In 1906, in place of the Gordon Bennett (about whose conditions they had rooted objections) the Automobile Club de France organized their first Grand Prix. The race, which occupied two days, was held on the Sarthe circuit and at once it became the *Grande Epreuve*. The winner in 1906 was the Hungarian, Szisz, in a Renault. At the last moment the wire wheels shown here were exchanged for artillery wheels with Michelin detachable rims. Without them the Renault would not have won.

293. This view of Pierry's Brasier at its depot in the 1906 Ardennes race gives a vivid impression of the earliest days of Grand Prix racing. The rear rims are being changed and fuel replenished with can and funnel. Note the exhaust manifolding of the car, the crude quick-lift jack and the screw jack carried on the chassis side member.

294. The Italian Challenge: Felic Nazzaro in the F.I.A.T. with which he won the 1907 Grand Prix a Dieppe averaging 70.5 m.p.h. fo $6\frac{3}{4}$ hours. He had finished secon the previous year.

295. Another Italian contender: Cagno's 1908 G.P. Itala weighs in for the Coupe Florio in which it finished third.

296. The 1908 Grand Prix on the Dieppe circuit dealt another mortal blow to French pride. The race marked the return of Germany to the field and it was won by a hitherto unknown driver, Christian Lautenschlager, in this Mercedes. Speed, 69 m.p.h. for 477.4 miles.

297. The Napier cars for the 1908 Grand Prix were barred by the A.C.F. because they were fitted with Rudge type quick detachable wheels which Rudge had used with success for his record run the previous year. Not unnaturally, this caused much ill feeling and Napiers never again entered for a continental race. Here is one of the 1908 G.P. cars later converted into a tourer.

298. Smarting from their defeat, French manufacturers induced their fellows to withdraw
official support from the Grand Prix and the
event languished until 1912. A desultory
formula libre event in 1911 was distinguished by
the appearance of the tiny Bugatti which was
driven into second place by Friderich, his
mechanic carrying the spare wheel for the whole
distance. So far as the 'giant racer' was concerned, the writing was upon the wall.

299-301. The 1912 Grand Prix at Diepp
marked the beginning of a new era a
represented by Georges Boillot (left) in th
twin overhead camshaft Henry-designe
Peugeot. The race saw a dramatic due
between Boillot and the old régime repre
sented by the immense F.I.A.T. driven b
the American, Bruce Brown. The Peuge
won. Below (left) the winner shoots unde
Eu Viaduct. Right: Gordon Crosby
on-the-spot impression of Bruce Brown i
full cry.

302. The result of the Coupe de L'Auto, which was run concurrently with the 1912 Grand Prix emphasized that the age of giants was at an end. The 3-litre side-valve Sunbeams not only finished first, second and third in the Coupe de L'Auto but third, fourth and fifth in the Grand Prix. The drivers are (l to r) Medinger, Dario Resta, Rigal and Caillois while Coatelen stands beside the trophies.

303. Two new racing Peugeots appeared for 1913, the 5.65-litre car in which Boillot won the French Grand Prix for the second time and the beautiful 3-litre for *voiturette* racing which was technically the most successful of all Henry-designed cars. Here is the 3-litre in action. Notice the 'knock off' hub caps—Boillot's time-saving idea.

04. High craftsmanship: the engine of the 1913 3-litre Peugeot.

305. Again in 1913 the Italian Grand Prix challenge failed. This vivid action picture shows Felice Nazarro cornering the rotary-valve Itala shortly before the chassis failed.

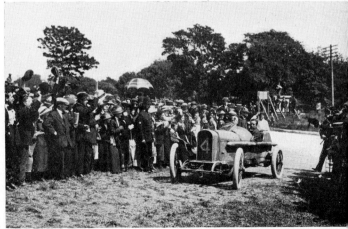

306-310. The last major British event before war broke out was the 1914 T.T. in the Isle of Man which was won by K. Lee Guinness, Sunbea
Our pictures show the animated scene before the start; the Vauxhall team cars; Hancock (Vauxhall) at Kirkmichael and (bottom) the wini
at Quarter Bridge and returning to the paddock after the race.

311-313. The 1914 French
Grand Prix at Lyons was one
of the most dramatic encounters
of all time. It marked the first
appearance, since 1908, of Mercedes, but the French were
confident that the invincible
Georges would again keep the
honours for France. His 1914
Peugeot (top, Rigal's car) had
Perrot-type front wheel brakes
and, in place of a bolster tank,
a long streamlined tail housing
vertically a spare wheel, which
is said to have upset the weight
distribution.

For the first time in racing
history the team of four Mercedes

[continued below

an to team orders signalled from their pit. Individual brilliance
was matched against planned strategy and lost. Boillot held the
lead until the penultimate lap but always the angular white
Mercedes remained within striking distance. On the last lap the
Peugeot broke a valve and Georges was led weeping from his
car. The story of 1908 was repeated; 'First, Lautenschlager,
Mercedes' (centre picture) but this time it was Mercedes second
and third also. The war clouds were heavy over Europe and the
Mercedes engine (right) was developed for war in the air. Not
long after, German machines shot down Georges Boillot, one
of the greatest drivers of France.

1914  1918

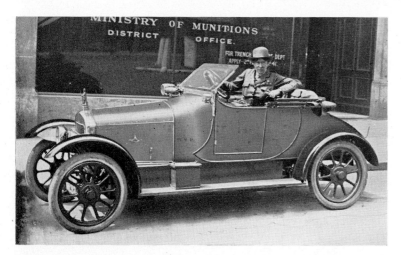 

315-317. A hot afternoon in that golden summer of 1914, the culmination of so many years of peace. European war seemed unthinkable or, if it came, it would surely be over in a few weeks. Yet the settled ease and assurance, the straw boater, the sun twinkling on the brass lamps, the somnolent sound of a distant lawn mower—these things belonged to a world that was ending. Soon that be-flowered hat and ankle-length skirt would change into the uniform of the W.V.R. while the car itself would be transformed into something frighteningly like those horrid machines that Mr Wells had been writing about.

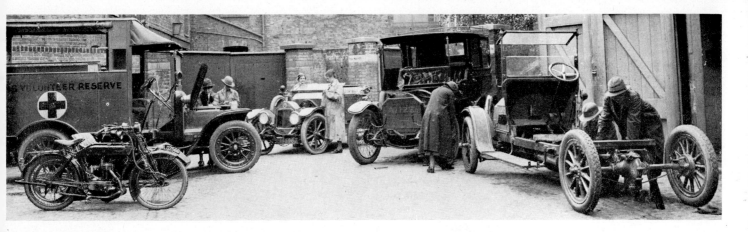

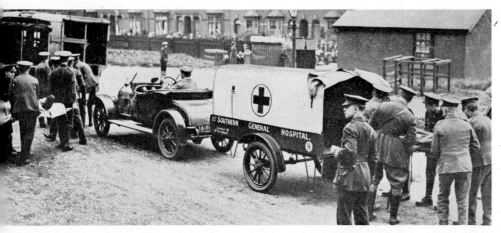

318/319. An emancipated generation of women manned garages and became mechanically minded while private cars were pressed into service to draw trailer ambulances.

320. One can imagine pleading to be left to die in peace rather than face being borne away in this fashion on a Bedelia cyclecar.

321/322. For the first time in history danger threatened from the skies so this Swift has its headlights partly blacked out. But in 1918 the terror, the years of mud and blood and agony, came to an end at last and a battered Europe faced the Twenties.

III

* Between the Wars *

BECAUSE the manufacture of motor cars practically ceased in Europe during the war years is not to say that designers and engineers were merely marking time. True, the first cars to be built after the war closely resembled their predecessors of 1914, but the demand for cars had to be met, while it takes time to put an entirely new design into production. When the true post-war models began to appear they revealed that many lessons had been learnt during the war particularly in the field of aero engine manufacture where considerations of minimum weight and maximum efficiency were all important. Thus the twenties saw the introduction of light, high-speed engines using overhead valves and making extensive use of light alloys and new high-tensile steels in place of the old slow-speed side-valve units. The new models had four wheel brakes, and by 1926 all new cars boasted front brakes, advertising the fact by a red triangle on the rear mudguard.

Nineteen hundred and nineteen saw the appearance of the first entirely original design—the Hispano Suiza, and it is hardly an exaggeration to describe it as inspired and prophetic, combining as it did in one superb chassis practically every feature which would distinguish the best engineering practice for the next decade. With its six-cylinder overhead camshaft engine, dropped chassis frame and large-diameter four-wheel brakes actuated by mechanical servo, this Hispano had that ageless quality which distinguishes only the highest craftsmanship.

But unfortunately the Hispano was a large luxury car, and in this country the tide of taxation was against such machines. The big Napiers and Lanchesters disappeared, newcomers to the class were commercially unsuccessful and even Rolls-Royce bowed to the storm to the extent of producing a 'Twenty'. On the other hand the light cars which had first been developed just before the war, and others like them, enjoyed a tremendous boom in the early twenties. And for the even more impecunious motorist there was still the cyclecar in diverse weird shapes as crude and unreliable as ever. But in 1922 the late Sir Herbert Austin produced his famous Austin 'Seven' and from that moment the cyclecars, and many of the less meritorious light cars, were doomed to extinction.

The twenties saw the appearance of a new type of car for whose genesis it is not easy to account since it had nothing to do with taxation. As they recede into history, the twenties spell for most people a kind of lost week-end, an interlude of reactionary folly which followed the rigours of the war and which came to an end in the harsh realities of the great slump and the rise of the dictators. It was the decade of the 'Flapper' with cloche hat and skirt above the knee, of the Charleston, the shingle and the Eton crop, of Michael Arlen and a youthful Noel Coward. Yet for the motoring enthusiast the twenties mean something entirely different; they mean the decade of the Vintage sports car, a period when 'bespoke' automobile engineering craftsmanship reached its peak. Before the war there had been 'fast touring cars' such as the 'Prince Henry' Vauxhall, but the sports car as such did not exist as a specific type. In fact, most of the owners of 'torpedo' touring cars before the war were enthusiasts and in the twenties, when the standard tourer became commoner, more staid and docile so that to drive it was no longer an adventure, the enthusiasts began to demand a car of fiercer metal. The manu-facturers' answer to this demand was a series of machines which were designed and built by craftsmen and which were distinguished by a high finish, a high performance and exemplary road manners. Their like had not been seen before and it would not be seen again when the 'Vintage Decade' was over.

With the light-car boom, traffic congestion became a problem for the first time and by the end of the decade the white line, the one-way street, traffic lights, parking restrictions and new by-pass roads had all made their appearance in England though not on a universal scale. But these measures were not able to keep pace with a motor industry which, in the early thirties, underwent the most significant revolution in its history. As a result of the great slump many firms went out of business while those which survived did so by adopting mass-production methods which had already been perfected in America. Unfortunately the new technique was not readily mastered. The designer was subordinated to the salesman and the production engineer with the consequence that during the thirties Britain turned out some of the worst cars ever made. They were short-lived, they were shoddy and they had disgraceful road manners. Their portraits do not appear in the following pages for it is best that they should be forgotten. They contributed greatly not only to road congestion but to road dangers. Their banality has tended to obscure such positive developments as the light, strong all-steel body and the fluid flywheel and pre-selector and synchromesh gearboxes which robbed the old 'crash' box of its terrors for the novice; likewise the widespread introduction of hydraulic and other improved braking systems.

Because the racing car can never be mass-produced, in this field no abyss divides the two decades and the story of motor racing between the wars is one of continuous and remarkable technical development. In 1922, 133 m.p.h. was the greatest speed ever recorded on land. In 1939 the world's flying kilometre record stood at 369.74 m.p.h. But this prodigious speed was achieved by a 'freak' car especially designed for this purpose alone. Much more significant from a technical point of view was the fact that by 1939 road racing cars of limited size and weight were capable of speeds in excess of 200 m.p.h. Such a speed means not merely tremendous strides in the power output of the internal combustion engine but, a fact of much greater importance, it means a vast improvement in chassis design, in suspension, brakes, and steering. Only thus could such terrific power be utilized, not on a special track but on a tortuous road circuit.

Volumes could be, and indeed have been devoted to the fascinating study of the development of the Grand Prix road racing car alone, and in the following pages there appear only a few of the more notable milestones along the road of this extraordinary development: the straight-eight Ballot, the first supercharged F.I.A.T., the brilliant $1\frac{1}{2}$-litre Delage, the famous 'monoposto' Alfa Romeo, and finally the revolutionary German Auto-Union and Mercedes-Benz. The latter, with their systems of independent suspension on all four wheels, introduced entirely new standards of road holding and made obsolete overnight the conventional chassis design which had persisted since the earliest days of motoring. Yet it is an interesting example of the continuity of motoring history that the layout of the Mercedes rear axle should incorporate a principle which was patented by the Count de Dion in 1894. Do not suppose that the road racing car is a freak machine. On the contrary it is the eternal prototype, the *avant garde* of motoring. Thus it is that the car of to-day embodies many of the lessons learned on the circuits of Europe between the wars.

324-329. So far as the vehicles are concerned, these pictures of Ascot traffic in 1920, and even the later view of Piccadilly, might have been taken before the war. But the Ascot fashions and cigarette-smoking student of form at Brooklands tell us we are in a new and scarcely becoming age.

330/335. As the cars of the 'twenties began to throng the roads, many now familiar phenomena appeared for the first time: the week-end trek to the seaside or to 'beauty spots' such as Runnymede or Newlands Corner. Radio found its way on to the motor-car as a prelude to being built-in and the trailer caravan appeared. What with one thing and another it became more and more difficult to find a track that was unbeaten.

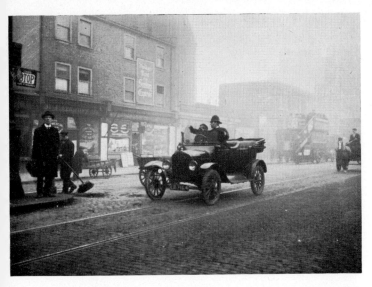

336/337. More traffic meant new means of control. This is not one of the Keystone Cops but a member of the London force controlling East End traffic. Right: the first white line, Whitehall, October 1924.

338/339. The complete stoppage of public transport caused by the General Strike of 1926 brought private cars into London in unprecedented numbers to provide a foretaste of traffic blocks and parking problems to come.

340/341. 1926 saw the first 'gyratory' traffic systems introduced at Hyde Park Corner and Piccadilly Circus.

342/343. More innovations of 1926: The now familiar 'One way street' sign at Hyde Park Corner and the first traffic signals (with control box) at the top of St. James's Street.

344/347. New roads on London's perimeter became vital. Top left: The Southend road, April 1925; Right: King George V opens the Great West Road, May 1925; Below, right: Stanley Baldwin opens the Kingston By-pass and the North Circular practically completed, 1926.

348. This illuminated white line installed at Hendon in 1925 anticipated our 'catseyes' by many years.

349. First experiments with radio communication for police cars, 1926.

350-351. More traffic meant more road accidents and to deal with these more effectively the first 'motor ambulances' made their appearance in 1925.

352-353. The wreck was borne off to a garage like this, displaying, in 1921, some of the first petrol pumps. Such garages had one amenity, now, alas, forgotten—the slot pump which supplied the belated motorist with a copious draught of petrol for his shilling.

354. Post-war Prototype: the chassis of the incomparable Hispano Suiza, 1919.

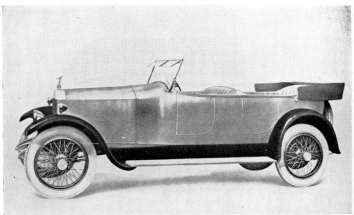

355-356. Messrs. Rolls-Royce had concentrated for so many years on the production of the 'Silver Ghost' alone, that the appearance of the first 'Twenty' in 1921 was a major sensation in the motoring world. Here it is in original open and closed forms.

357. Another sensation followed in 1924 when Derby announced the demise of the 'Silver Ghost'. It was succeeded by the o.h.v. 'New Phantom' the first Rolls to be fitted with front wheel brakes. Here Sir Henry Royce himself is seen at the wheel of one of the first 'Phantoms' at his home West Wittering in 1926.

58-361. Hail and Farewell: The appearance of the Twenty Rolls was a sign of the times. To an increasing extent economy motoring was the order of the day and the market for high powered cars became very limited. Newcomers to this class were the 8-litre Bentley and the Daimler 'double six', Britain's first 12-cylinder production car, but by the end of the 'twenties Napier and Lanchester had both ceased production, the latter surviving in name only.

362/366. The bonnet of the best products of the 'twenties concealed superb engineering craftsmanship. Top, left: The 40/50 Napier; Right: The generator of the American E Type Doble, the last word in steam cars. Below: The Leyland Eight and Isotta Frashini. Right: By contrast with these vintage interiors the bonnet of the modern car, like some chaotic odds and ends drawer, conceals a multitude of sins beneath a smooth exterior.

367-369. In the twenties the light car came into its own. Most popular and famous of all was the bull-nosed Morris Cowley (centre), a smaller and cheaper version of the pre-war Oxford. Bottom: The Clyno vied with the Cowley in popularity for a time, but the Wolverhampton firm over-reached themselves.

370-373. Light cars and cyclecars of the twenties. Top: The popular little Citroen, one of the first makes to introduce the new 'balloon' low-pressure tyres. Right: The stalwart flat-twin Jowett, a car with a record production life. Below: The Rover air-cooled twin 'eight' and the odd little two-stroke Carden which called itself the first £100 car. It gave you a lot of trouble for your money.

374. Epoch-making design: the 1922 Austin Seven. Like the pre-war Baby Peugeot, the Baby Austin was no crude cyclecar but a motor car in miniature giving remarkable value for money. It brought motoring within the reach of millions and killed the cyclecar.

375-376. Foretastes of the future: Some of the earliest streamlined saloons were evolved by the designers of rear-engined chassis, an arrangement then thought to favour such treatment. Here is the 1921 independently-sprung German Rumpler and (right) the British Burney.

377-378. Another British rear-engined car was the Crossley. Below: The Rosengart (a French-built version of the Austin Seven) anticipated the small car of to-day with its enveloping body and front cowling.

379-381. The Fabric Saloon. One reason why open cars held their popularity so long was the weight and expense of closed coachwork. Unless it was of top quality and massively built, the coach-built body soon racked itself to pieces. The Weymann fabric-covered body was a weight-saving solution popular in the years immediately prior to mass production. Here, on Lea Francis, Riley and Talbot chassis are three typical examples. Note the 'sunshine roof' on the Talbot. The Riley 'Nine' saloon was a revolutionary design when first introduced in 1926.

382-383. The era of mass-production introduced the pressed-steel body to England. It soon made obsolete the traditional methods of body building (top) and covered British roads with small saloon cars.

384. Not only British body building but the whole technique of car manufacture was revolutionized when American mass-production methods were applied.

385/386. Many of the first fruits of mass-production in Britain were deplorable, but these two examples from the Continent proved that good motor cars could be produced by such methods. Above: The front-wheel drive Citroen had admirable road manners. First introduced in 1932, the design is basically unchanged to-day. Left: Although poorly finished the F.I.A.T. '500' introduced in 1938 set a new standard of road holding and accurate steering in so small a car and could be called the prototype of the modern baby car.

387,388. Changes in Transmission.
Right: The 1929 Armstrong Siddeley was the first car to fit the Wilson pre-selector gearbox.
Below: Daimler carried the process a step further by combining the pre-selector gearbox with a fluid flywheel in place of the normal manual clutch.

389. The Fabulous Bugatti 'Royale'. Many enthusiasts deplored the eclipse of hand craftsmanship by the new machine methods. Among the few makers who did not yield to the new techniques Ettore Bugatti was outstanding. He continued to produce cars of true vintage quality until 1939.

390/391. When the new plants came into full production and began to pour their cars on to the roads of England the result, in the late thirties, was traffic congestion hitherto undreamed of. Here is the Rochester By-Pass on a fine summer week-end and Hyde Park Corner as it looked during the Jubilee celebrations of 1935.

THE VINTAGE SPORTS CAR

The Twenties represent the Golden Age of the 'Vintage' Sports Car. Here are some contemporary portraits of a few of the most celebrated.

92. The 30/98 Vauxhall Velox. The production version of Higginson's special car appeared in 1920. It had side valves whereas the later 'OE' type had push-rod O.H.V.

393. The old G.N. cycle-car with its chain drive took on a new lease of life as the Frazer Nash. Fitted with water-cooled four-cylinder side-valve Anzani engine it was a true enthusiast's mount.

4. Reliable but staid light cars had made the name of the Lagonda company since before the war, but in 1927 they caused a sensation when they dropped these sober manufactures and launched this 2-litre sports car with twin high-camshaft engine. It was the first of many successful sports cars.

395. After the war a new star appeared in the Coventry firmament—Alvis. At first the new firm built side-valve engines but in 1923 they produced the first of the o.h.v. '12/50' models as shown here in 'super-sports' form with 'duck's back' body. It was one of the most popular and long-lived of the smaller sports cars.

396. Lionel Martin built himself a special car in which he competed at Aston and other hill-climbs. Its success encouraged him to put it into production and the result was the Aston Martin, one of the most handsome of vintage machines.

397. In 1928 the Alvis Company put a front-drive sports car into production. This picture shows the prototype with a de Dion-type layout as used on the American Duesenberg employing a solid front axle. The production car had independent suspension but the inboard front brakes were retained.

398. This F.I.A.T. cockpit reveals the characteristic qualities of the vintage period: simplicity, solidity and good workmanship, with a complete absence of meretricious 'frills'

399. Cecil Kimber and the first M.G., 1923. When Kimber of Morris Garages built this first car its ancestry was obvious and endowed it with reliability rather than speed. But soon the M.G. would acquire a reputation of its own as one of the most successful midget sports cars of all time, its long list of successes culminating in the achievements of Captain Gardner's celebrated 'Magic Midget'.

oo. Besides these British ars, France and Italy nade many notable conributions to the Vintage anks. Technically, the nost significant of these mportations was the talian Lancia 'Lambda'. esides using from the rst a very fine system of ndependent front suspenon, Lancia was the first o consider the motor car s a single structure inead of as a chassis to rry a body. In Lancia's esign the 'body' became art of the chassis, thus nticipating modern esign.

1. Latecomer: Inspired by H. R. Godfrey (the 'G' of the G.N. partnership) the .R.G. which first appeared in 1935 was the last new car in the vintage tradition to built in England.

402. America, too, had her vintage period. This eight-cylinder Packard reveals the classic American line on the eve of its decadence.

403. After the war W. O. Bentley (whom we met in the last section driving a D.F.P.) and Burgess, who had designed the 1914 T.T. Humber, decided to build a sports car. The result was the 3-litre Bentley. In this picture 'W.O.' is at the wheel of one of the team of three cars which ran in the 1922 T.T., finishing second, fourth and fifth.

404. The 3-litre Bentley soon won its spurs at Brooklands. Here is W. G. Barlow's car after winning the 90 m.p.h. Short Handicap, August 1922. Behind him may be seen Scriven's Austin '20' and Cook's famous Vauxhall 'Rouge et Noir'.

405. By winning the famous twenty-four hour sports car race at Le Mans no less than five times (1924, 1927-1930) the Bentley greatly enhanced British prestige abroad at a time when Grand Prix racing was in eclipse. The 1927 victory was the result of one of the epic drives in motoring history. The Bentley team were involved in a sensational multiple crash from which only 'Old Number Seven' (her number the previous year) could be extricated. With damaged chassis and axle pushed back on the spring, the car was gallantly driven on and eventually won. In this picture, taken at the pit, the damage, including the misaligned axle, is revealed clearly. S. C. H. Davis has just handed over to his co-driver, Dr Benjafield, who is re-fuelling.

406. Le Mans, 1928 and victory for the 4½ Bentley driven by Barnato and Rubin.

407. Le Mans, 1929 and the peak of Bentley achievement. First the Speed Six (No. 1) driven by Birkin and Barnato with 4½ Bentleys in second, third and fourth positions.

408. The 1930 Le Mans saw this great combination in action—Sir Henry Birkin in the 'Blower 4½'. His epic duel with the Bentleys' most formidable opponent, Rudolph Caracciola in the supercharged 38/250 h.p. Mercedes, brought about its intended result, the retirement of the Mercedes and 6½-litre Bentleys filling first and second places. In the same year, Birkin drove this most unsuitable car, weighing over two tons, into second place in the French Grand Prix at Pau.

409/411. Although as cars became better reliability trials became tougher they were never mud baths for freak specials as they are to-day. Then any good light car or sports car stood an equal chance. Top, left: A competitor on Stonesdale Hill. Right: A locally-built Hampton assaults Nailsworth Ladder with a prodigious overburden. Below: A smart 12/50 Alvis picks its way over a 'chassis breaker'.

412. Although driven off the road by more refined machines, the immortal G.N. and, later, numerous 'Specials' of obvious G.N. ancestry, continued to be star performers in speed hill-climbs and sprints throughout our period. This fine action picture of Captain Frazer Nash and his famous 'Kim II' at South Harting conveys the unique thrill of these big twins at speed.

413. In 1926 Giveen, driving the ex-Mays Brescia Bugatti, temporarily lost control and charged the spectators at Kop Hill with fatal results. In consequence, hill-climbing on public roads was stopped.

414. Only Shelsley Walsh survived until the coming of Prescott in the late thirties. Here: C. M. Harvey in the Alvis broadsides on the S bend at Shelsley.

415. A typical scene in the twenties.

416. The Bank Holiday meetings were a popular family institution.

417. The start of a race, May 1923; 'Ebby' walks down a line of cars which includes Wolseley 'Moth' and 'Fifteen' and a 200 miles race Horstmann.

418. Brooklands continued to be the nurse of greatness. Here is a youthful Henry Segrave with his 1920 Brescia Bugatti. A 1914 Grand Prix Opel was another of his early mounts.

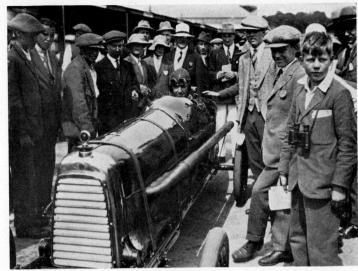

419-420. Of the many record breakers at Brooklands during the Twenties, the A.C. was perhaps the most outstandingly successful. It was the first light car to achieve 100 m.p.h. and finally raised the 1½-litre hour and 100 miles records to 104.19 m.p.h. Here an A.C. is seen leaping in the air after an attempt on the Brooklands test hill record. The famous 'Razor-blade' Aston Martin was built to challenge the A.C. but did not succeed due to a tendency to throw tyres.

421. Parry Thomas at work on the Leyland Eight. Designer, mechanic, consummate performer on the outer circuit, Parry Thomas was the greatest all-rounder that Brooklands ever produced. The Leyland, which was of his own original design, was phenomenally fast and ultimately recorded a lap at 129.36 m.p.h.

422. The 1½-litre eight-cylinder 'flat-iron' Thomas Special was another of Thomas's creations. In its lines and its ultra-low build it anticipates the racing cars of our own day.

423. Obsolete in road racing, the Brooklands outer circuit became the last thundering ground of the 'giant racer'. Here is the most popularly famous of all the latter-day giants—Count Zborowski's 'Chitty Bang Bang I'. It consisted of a six-cylinder 23,000 c.c. Maybach aero engine in a 75 h.p. Mercedes chassis.

424. Outstanding amongst the 'heavy metal' in the early thirties was Sir Henry Birkin in the single-seater 'Blower Bentley'. Birkin had many duels with Cobb on the twelve-cylinder Delage and ultimately raised the lap record to 137.96 m.p.h.

425. John Cobb and the Napier Railton. The big car tradition at Brooklands persisted until the end. With this car, which was specially built for the outer circuit, Cobb achieved the ultimate lap record figure of 143.44 m.p.h. in 1935.

426-427. Pit stop. Whereas attempts to simulate road-racing conditions at Brooklands were never successful, the 500 miles outer circuit race organized by the B.R.D.C. from 1929 onwards was a thrilling affair and robbed the Indianapolis '500' of the title of 'fastest race in the world'. Here Lord Howe brings his 3.3 Bugatti into his pit while his co-driver, the Hon. Brian Lewis, stands ready on the counter and the front of the car is already on the jacks for a wheel change. This 1935 race was won by Cobb on the Railton and to finish third Howe and Lewis averaged 115.03 m.p.h. Below: It is interesting to contrast the above example of carefully drilled and unflustered pitwork with this scene as Hancock makes a replenishment stop with the Vauxhall during a pre-war attempt on the world's twelve-hour record.

428/429. In 1933 the motoring world was astonished by the performance of a special 1½-litre supercharged Riley in the hands of Raymond Mays. With it he took the Shelsley record in this year. This Riley was the prototype of the E.R.A., the most successful road-racing car this country has so far produced. The E.R.A. had numerous victories at home and in 1½-litre events abroad. Below: Mays is seen taking the Shelsley record in 1939 with the 2-litre car with independent front suspension.

430. First post-war record breaker was K. Lee Guinness in the V12 350 h.p. Sunbeam who achieved 133.75 m.p.h. at Brooklands in May 1922. But in 1924 E. A. D. Eldridge in this immense 21.7-litre aero-engined F.I.A.T. 'Mephistopheles' raised the figure to 146.01 m.p.h. at Arpajon after a keen struggle with Rene Thomas's big Delage.

431. Malcolm Campbell now acquired the V12 Sunbeam and after unsuccessful attempts at Saltburn and in Denmark he succeeded in raising the record to 150.87 m.p.h. on Pendine Sands. Campbell was the first to use these sands where he is seen just before his successful run in 1925. After tyre-throwing troubles, Dunlops produced the first set of 'well base' wheels and tyres for this car.

432. Henry Segrave was next in the lists at Southport with the 4-litre V12 supercharged Sunbeam. He achieved 152.33 m.p.h. It was the last occasion on which the record would fall to a 'normal' motor car. Henceforth it would be the monopoly of monsters.

433-434. Parry Thomas acquired from Count Zborowski his Higham Special which was powered by a Liberty aero-engine of 26,907 c.c. Thomas modified the huge car, re-christened it 'Babs', took it to Pendine in April 1926 and put the record up to 171.02 m.p.h. Narrowly robbed of the record by Campbell's Napier-Campbell, Thomas tried again next year but tragedy intervened. Thomas was decapitated when a driving chain broke and the wreckage of 'Babs' was buried under the sands.

435. Magnificent failure. Having achieved the fabulous speed of 164 m.p.h. with a 1½-litre Miller, the American, Frank Lockhart, decided to attempt the world's speed record using two Miller engines totalling only 3 litres in his beautifully streamlined Black Hawk Stutz. On his first attempt a gust of wind caught the Stutz, it plunged into the sea and was badly damaged. Undaunted, Lockhart repaired the car and tried again. On his first run he recorded 203.45 m.p.h. On his second, the offside rear tyre burst and Lockhart lost his life in the fearful crash which followed. In 1928, this was a triumph of technical skill over brute force almost without parallel in motoring history. In our picture, Lockhart is seen at speed on Daytona beach shortly before disaster struck.

436. First at 200 m.p.h.: Segrave's twin-engined '1,000 h.p.' Sunbeam with which he achieved 203.79 m.p.h. at Daytona, March 1927.

437. First at 300 m.p.h.: Malcolm Campbell with his famous 'Bluebird' in its final form in which he achieved his ambition by raising the record to 301.13 m.p.h. on Bonneville Salt Pans in 1935.

438. The apotheosis of the 'giant racer': George Eyston's fantastic 'Thunderbolt' with steering by four-wheeled bogie and two blown Rolls-Royce engines totalling 73 litres and delivering 6,000 h.p. He raised the record to 357.5 m.p.h. in Utah in 1938.

439. The 1919 Henry-designed straight-eight Indianapolis Ballot. This was the first new road racing car to appear after the war and the first successful 'straight eight'. Although unlucky in competition it laid down the lines of post-war development.

440. The Straight-eight Duesenberg. In the first post-war French Grand Prix at Le Mans in 1921 America scored her only victory in a European *grande epreuve*. The race was won by J. Murphy's Duesenberg at 78.1 m.p.h. The car had water-operated hydraulic brakes, the first time hydraulic brakes had been seen in Europe.

441. In 1922 F.I.A.T. won the French Grand Prix with a six-cylinder 2-litre car weighing only 14 cwt which marked a significant break-away from the Henry school of design. In 1923 this car was re-designed as a super-charged straight-eight as shown in our picture. It was the first supercharged car to win a Grand Prix (the Italian) and the first to compress mixture instead of forcing air through the car-burettor as was done by Chadwick and Mercedes. Henceforth no unsuper-charged car would win a Grand Prix.

442/443. Humphrey Cook in his 1922 3-litre T.T. Vauxhall. With four-cylinder twin o.h.c. Ricardo-designed engine developing 130 h.p. at 4,500, this was the most advanced design produced in Britain during the twenties. But alas, the car never had a chance to show its metal on the Continent, having been built in blissful ignorance of the fact that from 1922 onwards the G.P. formula limited capacity to 2 litres. The Vauxhall took many class records and later one of them (right) became the 'Villiers Supercharge', an immensely successful sprint car driven by Mays and Cummings.

444. Segrave cornering in the victorious 2-litre Sunbeam, French Grand Prix, Tours, 1923. Britain's only French Grand Prix victory and the last occasion on which the race was won by an unsupercharged car.

445. Both the French and Italian Grand Prix in 1924 were won by a new and formidable name—Alfa Romeo. Here is the 165 b.h.p. supercharged straight-eight 2-litre 'P2' Alfa with Campari at the wheel on the occasion of the 1925 French Grand Prix at Montlhery. Campari was in the lead when he withdrew after his team-mate Ascari had crashed fatally and the race was won by the 2-litre Delage.

446. The start of the Coupe des Voiturettes, Boulogne, 1925. Although Britain was represented in Grand Prix racing only by the Sunbeam-Talbot-Darracq combine, she featured much more prominently in voiturette racing throughout our period. In this view G.N. and Frazer Nash are well to the fore. The race was won by a Frazer Nash driven by Clive Gallop.

447-448. The middle twenties brought two changes: A 1½-litre Grand Prix formula and the abolition of the intrepid riding mechanic. How unhappy his lot had become in the cause of reducing frontal area is revealed in our picture. The 1926 F.G.P. at Miramas was a walk-over for Bugatti, no other cars being ready, but thereafter the 1½-litre straight-eight Delage designed by M. Lory proved absolutely unbeatable. The Delage was one of the most complex yet successful designs of all time and when ten years old it decisively defeated modern E.R.A.s in the hands of Dick Seaman. It is here seen in a place of honour at the Paris salon after its triumphant 1927 season.

449. 'Le Patron': Ettore Bugatti, one of the most gifted automobile designers in the history of the motor car. He was the only manufacturer who built racing cars on a limited production basis. Consequently, when Grand Prix racing sank into the doldrums after 1927 for lack of manufacturer support and formula libre became the rule, Bugatti cars were soon supreme in Europe. Altogether the type 51 and type 35 Bugattis won thirty-three major road races in seven years.

450. Bugatti won the French Grand Prix for three years in succession. Here is one of the greatest French drivers of our period, Louis Chiron, in his Type 51 after winning the 1931 ten-hour event at Montlhery at an average of 78.16 m.p.h.

451. 'Mantovano Volante' Tazio Nuvolari is generally considered the greatest racing driver of all time. He drove many cars but his memory will always be associated with the equally famous P 3 'mono-posto' Alfa Romeos of the Scuderia Ferrari. The P3 might be called the last word in traditional racing cars, and between 1931 and 1934 it became practically unassailable, its only serious challenger being the Maserati.

452. Winner of the Irish Grand Prix, 1933 and of the Ulster T.T., Rudolph Caracciola, Mercedes-Benz. Until 1934 Germany made only occasional appearances in international road races. Her most polished driver was Caracciola whose handling of the unwieldy 38/250 h.p. SSK Mercedes on a wet road was incredible to behold. But by 1933 rumours of fabulous new cars were in the air. . . .

453-455. From 1934 onwards, road racing in Europe was increasingly dominated by the new Auto-Union and Mercedes-Benz racing cars which, with their independent suspension, revolutionized the sport. Enthusiasts too impecunious to see the cars on foreign circuits will never forget the Donnington Grand Prix of 1937 pictured here. Left: Pike and minnows: Caracciola, Mercedes, pursues two E.R.A.s at Red Gate. Centre and bottom: The cars leap in the air as they accelerate up the slope from Melbourne corner. No more powerful road racing cars have ever been built, the Mercedes in its final form developing 646 b.h.p. at 5,500 r.p.m.

456. Teutonic craftsmanship: the sixteen-cylinder engine of the C type rear-engined Auto Union which was so successful in 1936-7 in the hands of Berndt Rosemeyer. B.h.p. 520 at 5,000 r.p.m., speed 175 m.p.h.

457. Caracciola wins the German Grand Prix at Nurburg-ring in the new 3-litre formula Mercedes-Benz. More controllable than the earlier 750 kg. formula cars, the new Mercedes was equally fast and was quite unbeatable in 1938/9. As the war clouds gathered and the low white Mercedes flashed unconquerably round the circuits of Europe, history repeated itself and men remembered the French Grand Prix at Lyons in 1914.

458. In streamlined form, Caracciola's 3-litre Mercedes-Benz covered the flying mile at 248 m.p.h. in 1939.

Epilogue

AT THIS MOMENT of writing ten years have gone by since the Second World War ended. Imagine for a moment that we are back in the year 1928, ten years after the First World War. How fairly could we have assessed the motoring developments of that past decade or forecast what changes we should see in the decade to come? Surely we should have been very wide of the mark. How much greater then the possibility of error to-day when progress in the last ten years has been even more bewilderingly rapid. When, in 1939, we saw supercharged Grand Prix racing cars capable of exceeding 200 m.p.h. it seemed that development could scarcely go further. Yet to-day we have unsupercharged production sports cars capable of exceeding 150 m.p.h.

Concerning the past decade of motoring history, certain significant facts do emerge quite clearly and indisputably. First, although the 'Vintage' motorist may very properly shake his head over the quality of workmanship and finish it displays and its general inaccessibility, he can scarcely deny that the average mass-produced motor car of to-day is an altogether different and better proposition than its predecessor in the 1930s. It not only performs better but it steers more accurately, has better brakes, better road-holding and cornering and has a better driving position which provides an excellent un-obstructed view ahead. In its use of independent suspension and in other details it reveals the fact that the designer is returning to his rightful pre-eminence and that

146

through him the lessons learned on the racing circuit are now more quickly applied.

Second, although given two engines of similar design and capacity, the super-charged unit is still the superior, the most significant feature of engine development since the war has been the increase in the power output of 'unblown' engines. It is this development which has given the present day sports car so phenomenal a performance; this combined with a good power/weight ratio (a factor sadly ignored since the early twenties) and streamlining. That the high speeds of which these present-day cars are capable should be virtually unattainable in this country owing to chronic traffic congestion is a paradox with a moral which need not be laboured here.

The third feature which distinguishes the past decade has been the tremendous increase in the public interest both in motor racing and in the motoring past. This became apparent so soon as motoring events began to be held again after the war. Before the war those of us who raced motor cars or nursed ancient veterans were often made to feel that we were a small and eccentric minority indulging in a pastime almost as far removed from popular interest as archery or that variety of tennis which is not played on lawns. We used to deplore the apathy of the general public to motor sport in those days but now, such is our inconsistency, we sometimes sigh nostalgically for those old informal, friendly days now that motor racing draws immense crowds and any assembly of veteran cars is swamped by hordes of interested spectators. It is possible for the sport to suffer from too much patronage as well as from neglect, so whether the outcome of this new interest will be good or bad cannot be forecast. Motor sport can become too commercialized and exclude the true but impecunious enthusiast, but, on the other hand, without the public interest which has always existed on the Continent, Grand Prix racing could never have continued.

With Donnington Park lost and Brooklands shamefully sold, the prospect before the sport immediately after the war looked very dark, and this absence of motor-racing courses would have been bad for our motor industry as well as for the sport. Yet now we have more circuits in this country and a fuller calendar than ever before. It is a direct result of this renaissance of the sport in England that British cars have acquitted themselves so well at Le Mans and in other sports car events abroad, building up a reputation which they have not held since the Bentley days.

And what of the future? What cars will appear on those blank walls of our picture gallery reserved for the nineteen sixties and seventies? The historian falls silent. He can only repeat the old truism that the racing car of to-day is the touring car of tomorrow and point to such features as the disc brake as an answer to the problem of stopping ultra-fast cars and to petrol injection which might ultimately relegate the carburettor to a case in the Science Museum. At this point he throws an apprehensive glance in the direction of the Gas Turbine and wonders whether the whole internal combustion engine as we know it may not become a museum exhibit before the century is out. Speaking with many voices, the piston engine has accompanied us through all the pages of this book, the moving spirit of the road revolution: the asthmatic wheeze and 'tuff' of the single-cylinder De Dion, the high-bred murmur of the 'Silver Ghost', the thunder of the 'giant racer' and the ear-splitting snarl of the Bugatti. For good or ill it has become a part of our lives and because the historian inevitably becomes a traditionalist he hopes and believes that a power unit so willing, so diverse in form and character from the staid and reliable to the brilliant and temperamental, will not be outmoded in his lifetime.

461. As in World War I, car manufacturers the world over had turned to war production between 1939 and 1945. But when peace returned cars by the thousand were soon rolling off the assembly lines with the result that today traffic problems are far more acute than they were in 1939.

462-463. Automatic drive: The pre-selector gear-box on the 1929 Armstrong Siddeley was only a step towards a goal to which designers have been moving for years—a fully-automatic gear-box which would eliminate the clutch pedal. Now, on the Continental Bentley (top) and the Armstrong Siddeley Sapphire this goal has been achieved.

464. Car of the future? This Gas Turbine Rover was the first car in the world to be fitted with this entirely new form of motive power.

465. The start of the 1948 British Grand Prix at Silverstone. This was the first Grand Prix to be organized by the R.A.C. since 1927. The vastly increased public interest in motor racing was first revealed at this event by the unprecedented crowds which flocked to the course. The race was won by Luigi Villoresi in a 1½-litre supercharged Maserati.

466. The 500 c.c. or Formula III racing car is an entirely post-war phenomenon. From the small beginning of a few home-built cars, Formula III racing has now become a popular feature at international meetings and the cars are built on a commercial scale. This picture shows the start of a '500' race at Goodwood, another post-war circuit which helped to fill the gap left by the tragic demise of Brooklands.

467. Four hundred miles an hour: The late John Cobb and his Railton Special. Just before war broke out, Cobb had raised the land speed record to 369.74 m.p.h. in Utah. In 1947 he returned to record the astonishing figure of 394.196 m.p.h. which still stands. His speed in one direction was 403.135 m.p.h. Powered by two 1929 supercharged Napier Lion engines driving all four wheels, the Railton represents a breakaway from the huge 'giant racer' of which the *Thunderbolt* was the last and largest example.

468. 'Hope deferred. . . .' No British car had carried Britain's colours in Grand Prix racing since the retirement of the Sunbeam-Talbot combine from road racing in the twenties, and in 1950 the hopes of all enthusiasts were centred on the long-awaited B.R.M. The most complex and, in theory, the most efficient road racing car ever designed, the B.R.M. never fulfilled expectations.

469-470. Perhaps the most remarkable of post-war developments has been the vastly increased power output of unsupercharged engines. This has been brought about by better 'breathing'. Left: The 'lungs' of the 4½-litre Ferrari. Above: The D Type competition Jaguar which was second at Le Mans in 1954 and succeeds the twice victorious C Type. The D Type has a maximum in excess of 170 m.p.h. and is the first British car in series production to be fitted with disc brakes.

471. Again Mercedes: In 1954, Mercedes made yet another spectacularly successful return to Grand Prix racing by finishing first and second in the French Grand Prix at Rheims. Here Stirling Moss, one of the most brilliant of Britain's post-war drivers, tries out the 1955 Mercedes. When shall we provide him with a car equally worthy of his skill?

*"In my end is my beginning": these pictures are typical of the immense interest shown today
in cars which represent the living history of motoring*

472. 'Veteran':
Decauville, Lanchester and Oldsmobile take part in a run organized by the Veteran Car Club of Great Britain.

473. 'Edwardian':
The line-up for an Edwardian Handicap Race at a Vintage Sports Car Club meeting at Silverstone. Among the starters are two early Grand Prix cars, a 1907 F.I.A.T., 1908 Itala (see picture 282) and 1914 T.T. Sunbeam.

474. 'Vintage':
Invicta, Lancia Lambda, Frazer Nash and a pride of Bentleys are among the starters in this race for vintage sports cars at Castle Combe.

INDEXES

For convenience, references have been divided into Cars, Drivers and General. In each Index italic numerals refer to page numbers; bold numerals refer to illustrations; and roman numerals refer to references in the captions to illustrations.

INDEX TO CARS

INDEX TO DRIVERS

GENERAL INDEX

ACKNOWLEDGMENTS

Author and Publisher express their grateful thanks to the following who supplied pictures for this History:

Agence Rol, 4, Rue Richer, Paris, for No. 451.

Armstrong Siddeley Motors, Ltd., for No. 463.

The Autocar, for Nos. 66, 105, 111, 122, 123, 124, 130, 132, 140, 141, 142, 146, 148, 149, 150 to 164, 167, 173, 176, 180, 181, 184, 196, 198, 199, 211, 230, 232, 235, 243, 244, 247, 250, 251, 259, 261, 264, 265, 268, 278, 293, 296, 297, 298, 299, 301, 315 to 321, 367, 368, 369, 382, 385 to 389, 401, 436, 438, 448.

The *Automobil Review* for No. 456.

Mr R. Barker for Nos. 126, 136, 360, 362.

Mr H. Austin Clark, Jun., Long Island, New York for No. 274.

Corrada Millanta, via Tarchetti, Milano for Nos. 313, 470.

Daimler Motors, Ltd for Nos. 134, 137, 359, 388.

Mr S. C. H. Davis for No. 405.

Mr Peter S. de Beaumont, 36, Cutler St., Connecticut for No. 280.

France Reportage, 14, Rue de Rome, Paris, 8, for Nos. 276, 292, 303, 304, 305, 444, 446.

Mr Guy Griffiths for Nos. 473, 474.

Jaguar Cars, Ltd for No. 469.

Mr Charles B. King, Larchmont, New York for No. 77.

Mr George Monkhouse for No. 457.

Mr J. E. S. Morley for No. 402.

The Motor for Nos. 28, 62, 71, 73, 78, 85, 86, 202, 263, 270, 302, 330, 331, 332, 333, 335, 346, 363, 364, 365, 366, 370, 371, 372, 375, 376, 377, 378, 380, 393 to 400, 403, 406 to 414, 418, 419, 422, 423, 424, 425, 426, 428, 429, 439, 440, 442, 443, 445, 449, 453, 454, 455, 458.

Mr St John Nixon for No. 61.

The *Picture Post* Library for Nos. 1 to 16, 21 to 27, 29 to 43, 45, 46, 50 to 54, 57 to 60, 65, 67, 68, 72, 79 to 83, 87 to 102, 104, 107 to 110, 114 to 121, 125, 127, 128, 129, 131, 133, 135, 138, 139, 144, 145, 147, 166, 172, 174, 175, 177, 178, 179, 182, 185 to 193, 195, 197, 200, 201, 203 to 210, 212 to 229, 231, 233, 234, 236 to 242, 245, 249, 252, 253, 254, 262, 266, 269, 271, 272, 273, 275, 277, 281 to 291, 294, 300, 306 to 310, 312, 314, 322 to 329, 334, 336 to 345, 347 to 354, 361, 373, 374, 379, 381, 383, 384, 390, 391, 404, 415, 416, 417, 421, 427, 430 to 435, 437, 447, 452, 459, 460, 461, 465 to 468, 471.

Mr H. P. Powell for No. 472.

M. Marius Prieur, 5, Rue Cambon, Paris for Nos. 106, 246, 256, 257, 258, 260, 295, 441.

Rolls-Royce, Ltd for Nos. 112, 267, 355, 356, 357, 462.

Rover Cars, Ltd for No. 464.

The Smithsonian Institution, Washington for Nos. 75, 76, 248, 279.

Vauxhall Motors, Ltd for Nos. 143, 392.

Wide World Photos, 106, Rue Reaumer, Paris for No. 450.

In a few cases it has not been possible to trace with certainty the sources of the pictures. Apologies are due for any omissions or errors in ascription which, despite every care, are liable to occur in the collection of so much historical material.